Christian Symbols
in a World Community

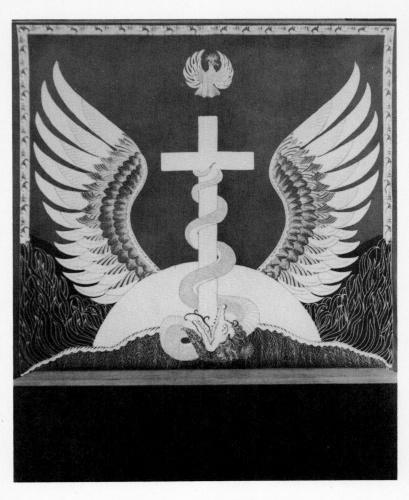

AN EAST JAVA REREDOS

FOR A DESCRIPTION OF THE SYMBOLISM SEE No. 222

Christian Symbols

IN A WORLD COMMUNITY

BY DANIEL JOHNSON FLEMING

UNION THEOLOGICAL SEMINARY · NEW YORK

FRIENDSHIP PRESS · NEW YORK

Companion Art Volumes by Daniel Johnson Fleming

HERITAGE OF BEAUTY

being pictorial studies of modern Christian architecture in Asia and Africa illustrating the influence of indigenous cultures.

EACH WITH HIS OWN BRUSH

with sixty-five reproductions of contemporary Christian paintings and carvings in Asia and Africa.

Also by the Same Author

BUILDING WITH INDIA

HELPING PEOPLE GROW

VENTURES IN SIMPLER LIVING

WHITHER BOUND IN MISSIONS

WAYS OF SHARING WITH OTHER FAITHS

ETHICAL ISSUES CONFRONTING WORLD CHRISTIANS

DEVOLUTION IN MISSION ADMINISTRATION

CONTACTS WITH NON-CHRISTIAN CULTURES

SCHOOLS WITH A MESSAGE IN INDIA

ATTITUDES TOWARD OTHER FAITHS

MARKS OF A WORLD CHRISTIAN

This volume could not possibly be sold at the price listed except as the result of a generous subsidy from a friend of the younger churches whose name is withheld by request. This volume and the other volumes in the same series, *Heritage of Beauty* and *Each with His Own Brush,* have been produced on a non-profit basis by author and publisher.

Foreword

Whenever Christian art of an original or high order begins to appear in any area it is a matter for rejoicing. Increasingly symbolic representations, adopted or adapted from Western or local cultures, are to be found in Asia, Africa and the Near East.

> Thus every artist paints Thee as his own
> Limned on the background of his time and thought;
> Set in the space which his life has known;
> Decked in the clothing which his hand has wrought.

The first objective of this study has been a factual inquiry—to ascertain and to illustrate the extent to which indigenous symbolism has been incorporated in Christian use and to discover the meanings assigned to such symbolism. Throughout there has been the attempt to see the problems and dangers as well as the values in the silent witness of wood and stone, especially when that witness is by means of indigenous forms. It is hoped that this survey of what has already been done may stimulate many churches and schools to express themselves creatively in forms that are part of their nation's heritage. A still broader purpose has been to demonstrate through specific illustrations that in an intelligent, constructive use of meaningful art forms there are values for religious education, meditation and worship that are deeper far than mere decoration. Underlying all has been the hope that a sympathetic introduction to one's neighbor's symbols would deepen the sense of world community.

There are many books dealing with the traditional Christian symbolism of the West. But so far as the author knows this is the first attempt to collect examples of the symbolic Christian art developing in Asia, Africa and the Near East. For the most part, these examples are the result of individual initiative and have to be separately discovered as isolated local efforts. This limited collection, therefore, does not pretend to be exhaustive. It is rather typical of one kind of expression in the much larger field of the naturalization and indigenization of Christianity. It is hoped that the study may provide a basis for an appraisal of what has already been done, and for some suggestions for guidance for the future.

Naturally each institution has its own interpretation of the symbols used. This accounts for a certain variation in the meanings associated with any given design.

The least valuable use that can be made of this book is a casual turning of the pages out of mere curiosity for strange art forms. For obviously many of the illustrations derive their value, not from their merit as designs of high art, but from the meanings associated with them—meanings that may be conjectured by the reader, and then checked from the accompanying descriptions.

A more creative use would be for a group to discuss, for example, what symbolism should be put on a lectern, or reading desk for the Scriptures, for which, in imagination, they were planning. When a Chinese was asked what he would choose, he thought the Bible might well rest on a representation of the five sacred mountains in China. An Indian, near whose home is a famous rock, thought his Bible might well rest on a representation of this rock as symbolic of what the Bible is—a strong foundation. Another, thinking of a gushing spring in Kashmir, would have springs of living water carved upon the lectern. How others have laid aside the eagle with outstretched wings, so common in the West, for a design of their own may be seen from the index under "lectern." Obviously, any other item in chancel furnishings could be planned; or meaningful symbols for a chapel doorway could be devised, either simply as an exercise in artistic and religious creativeness or with the intent of bringing about such changes as those described in illustrations Nos. 91 and 92. Again, just for example, the communion table in No. 128 embodies a suggestion of the ecumenical church; this could raise the question as to what other symbolism for this conception could be devised.

The seals and shields of schools and colleges introduce one to a surprising amount of local geography, history or aspiration. We learn about the lost book of the Karens in No. 62; we catch the detailed spirit and purpose of a seminary in No. 63; we see how the common, heart-shaped paddle of Kashmir embodies a permanent ideal in No. 71, and how ordinary piano keys are used to represent interracial cooperation in No. 193; a new symbol for the missionary spirit is developed in No. 55; and Nos. 72 and 172 show how rich

vi

meanings in a college shield may pervade an institution. Possibly a perusal of the two score examples of crests and shields of varying artistic merit and inner meanings may stimulate more creative work in devising institutional emblems of real beauty and significance.

One could survey the illustrations of this volume with the purpose of definitely rejecting any that seem inappropriate or unwise. But believing, in general, that each nation has something to contribute to the good of all, one might, also, discriminatingly select any that commend themselves, either as locally appropriate or as worthy of the Church Universal.

Perhaps the deepest gain would be the development of a planetary rather than a parochial or sectarian consciousness. The Christian fellowship is still a world minority—and yet it is the greatest influence making for unity that mankind possesses. If these Christian symbols, wrought out in different cultures and by different peoples, can help us to an appreciative understanding of other Christian groups and to a realization of our underlying unity, one main object of the volume will have been accomplished. This is a day when each Christian, everywhere, should permit a sense of the world-wide Christian community to become a reality in his life.

Acknowledgments

THE AUTHOR gratefully acknowledges help from literally hundreds who painstakingly gave the information which made the discovery and the description of these symbols possible. For the pictures themselves he is indebted as follows:

India: 7, Miss H. F. Greenfield; 8, Rev. M. H. Harrison; 9, 28-33, Rev. R. W. Stopford; 10, Mrs. H. Lester Smith; 12, Miss Eleanor Rivett; 19, Rev. Geo. Van B. Shriver, Rev. Philip B. Curtis; 20, Miss Eleanor D. Mason; 21-26, 48, Dr. S. Jesudason; 27, Dr. F. H. Gravely, Madras Museum; 34-38, Rev. G. E. Hubbard; 39, 40, A. Thomas, artist; 41, Dr. Reba C. Hunsberger; 42, Rev. J. H. Davey; 43, Rev. L. P. Jayaprabhu; 44-47, Mrs. L. D. Honegger.

China: 1-5, 114, Rev. F. J. M. Cotter and Mr. Walter A. Taylor; 13, Miss Margaret E. Barnes; 73, 84, 85, Miss Mabel S. Jones; 74-80, reprinted by permission of the President and Fellows of Harvard College; 81-83, Dr. Daniel Sheets Dye; 86-90, Dr. Karl Reichelt; 91, 92, Rev. Ernest T. Shaw and Miss Hazel F. Bailey; 93-95, 119, Rt. Rev. R. O. Hall Bishop of Hongkong; 96-101, Dr. H. H. Whitlock and Rev. Geo. C. Hood; 102-112, 115, Mr. Chas. T. Gee and Mrs. Paul DeWitt Twinem; 113, 121, Rev. Chas. A. Stanley; 116, 124, 125, Associated Boards for China Colleges; 117, 118, "Liturgical Arts" through Mr. Maurice Lavanoux; 120, Rev. Hugh Bousman; 126, Catholic University, Peiping; 127, 128, Rev. Arthur O. Rinden; 129-133, Dr. Robt. F. Fitch; 221, Catholic University, Peiping, through Miss Marie Adams; designs on page 76 from the Digest of Synodal Commission, Peiping, through Fr. Lawrence Bultmann.

Japan: 138-145, Miss Mary McDonald; 146-155, Rev. P. A. Smith; 156, 157, Rev. C. P. Garman; 158-166, 173, Rev. V. W. Peters; 174, 175, Miss Virginia McKenzie.

Africa: 176, 177, Miss A. M. Locke; 178, 179, Rev. W. J. Payne; 180, Rev. E. G. Wyatt; 181, 182, L. A. Creedy; 183, Principal Alexander Kerr; 184, 185, Miss Margaret Trowell; 186, Fides Foto; 187, Dr. Julius Richter and the Staatliches Museum für Völkerkunde; 188-191, Sister Pauline, C. R.; 192, Ev.-Luth. Mission zu Leipzig.

Near East: 199, 200, Rev. R. N. Sharp and Rev. C. H. Allen; 201, Rev. W. M. Miller and Dr. J. Christy Wilson; 203, Dr. C. R. Watson and Mr. Herman A. Lum; 205, Rev. J. R. Richards.

Miscellaneous: Frontispiece, 219, 220, 222, Rev. S. C. Graf van Randwijck; 11, Dr. Eugene C. Carder; 14-18, 215-218, Rev. Galen R. Weaver; 204, Rev. Geo. M. Gibson; 212-214, Rev. Takai Okumura.

The diocesan seals came directly from their respective dioceses, and the school and college crests from their corresponding institutions.

Contents

Part I : Values and Dangers in Symbols

For the invisible things of him since the creation of the world are clearly seen, being perceived through the things that are made, even his everlasting power and divinity.

ROMANS V:20

I : Weaving Christianity into the Cultural Tapestry

The Church Universal welcomes, rather than deprecates, the way in which each people cultivates traditions and tendencies based upon its own individual character—so long as they are consistent with essential Christianity. This need not dull the consciousness of universal brotherhood, nor endanger the sense of the unity of mankind. Strikingly significant, in this connection, is the way in which the findings and recommendations of what, geographically, was the most widely representative Christian gathering ever held repeatedly urged the recognition and use of values in indigenous cultures. The world meeting of the International Missionary Council at Tambaram, India, in 1938, made the following statements:

> We strongly affirm that the gospel should be expressed and interpreted in indigenous forms, and that in methods of worship, institutions, literature, architecture, etc., the spiritual heritage of the nation and country should be taken into use. The gospel is not necessarily bound up with forms and methods brought in from the older churches. . . . There are valuable cultural elements which ought to be preserved and integrated into the life of the new Christian community from its very beginning. An adequate understanding of the religions will recognize in them the presence of such valuable elements, side by side with other elements which are wholly opposed to the Christian revelation. . . . The inner life of worship becomes incarnate in words and acts and in the wordless speech of architecture and the other arts. . . . We would urge upon missionaries the duty of helping the younger churches to express their Christian life in forms that are part of their nation's heritage. (*The World Mission of the Church,* pp. 45, 55, 57.)

Each country has its own artistic language, as well as its verbal tongue; each people has traditional forms in which religious feeling has been embodied. Christianity, therefore, while still remaining catholic, must speak a language that men accustomed to these old forms can understand. Hence it is not alone the Scriptures that must be translated, but Christian thought and aspiration must find expression in meaningful art forms. It is not primarily the culture of

3

Western Christendom that is to be shared, but the witness of the eternal Christ, who will appropriately clothe himself by assimilating kindred elements from indigenous cultures. Increasingly, therefore, nationals themselves are asking what contribution indigenous arts can bring to the service of the Christ.

Great and exacting is the spiritual task of presenting Christian truth in art forms that will not, on the one hand, make Christianity seem foreign to a given people or, on the other, distort it by entanglement with non-Christian forms. Some of the difficulties and the dangers as well as the hopefulness of this task become apparent as these pages are turned. One could arrange all the illustrations in this book along some such scale of increasing departure from Western forms as the following:

I. Some have felt it safest to adhere strictly to the classical symbolism of the West. The cross is the outstanding example of this type; and rightly so, for it is preeminently significant and characteristic of the Christian faith. A suggestion of its universality as a Christian symbol, as well as of the ecumenical nature of Christianity, is found in the pictures of Part II.

II. One step out from this is placing a Western Christian symbol against a distinctively indigenous background. For example, a missionary architect of Peiping says that his organization has been more occupied with using accepted Christian symbolism in a Chinese way than with using actual Chinese symbolism. The general design may be preserved; but in place of the dragon, lotus and swastika are substituted the cross, vine and breastplate. Even at this second stage, however, non-Christian stone masons who may be executing the actual work very often diffuse into their product something that is delightfully Indian or Chinese. One can tell at once that the execution was not done in the West; that the symbol has passed through a Chinese or Indian medium. In this way even a Western model is rendered in an indigenous style. The entire terrace balustrade of St. Andrew's Church (Episcopal), Wuchang, alternates columns showing the Paschal Lamb and St. Andrew's Cross (the latter in accord with the name of the church). These symbols are set in a carved background or "cloud base," signifying everlasting. A cross with the grapevine pattern is in the lattice of each window. (See Nos. 1-5.)

4

1. ST. ANDREW'S CHURCH, WUCHANG

2. THE BALUSTRADE

3. ST. ANDREW'S CROSS

4. WINDOW LATTICE

5. PASCHAL LAMB

III. Some indigenous symbols, especially those on the shields or seals of colleges or dioceses, are mainly geographical. They show, however, that these Christian institutions are not naïvely Western, but wish to indicate in some way that they are rooted in the soil and are identifying themselves with the land in which they find themselves. For example, in the seal of Lingnan University, Canton, the

6. SEAL OF LINGNAN UNIVERSITY

college buildings are suggested on the right and left. Between is the main esplanade going down to the Pearl River, on which a ship floats by. In the background is White Cloud Mountain, a well-known hill near Canton.

IV. A more creative step is taken when quite new symbols are evolved growing out of the local culture, though not previously associated with any non-Christian religion. Thus, since in certain parts of Africa it is the custom for a leader to go ahead on a jungle path and take upon himself the dew, Christ as "dew-man" becomes a symbol. In No. 55 we see the banyan tree, whose branches have a way of dropping roots to the ground so that branches extend widely in all directions—a symbol of the missionary expansion that should characterize the church. In No. 101 the steep ascent of a mountain path is used to portray the Christian life. In No. 7 (next page) is another symbol growing out of the local environment, viz., the badge of the Church of Scotland Mission Girls' High School, Madras. Burdens are commonly carried on the head in South India. In order to rest the burden bearers, stone shelves have been erected here and there along the dusty highways. This common roadside institution has been taken as a symbol by this school, and is explained each year to incoming students by a school service which in part reads:

7. CHRIST, THE BURDEN BEARER

SENIORS: Our ideals can be seen in our badge—the burden bearer of the poor.

NEW GIRLS: What does it mean?

SENIORS: It means many things.

FIRST SENIOR: It stands upright, to show that we must be truthful and honest and fearless.

SECOND SENIOR: It stands firm to show that we must be strong in body and mind, so that we may be able to endure the storms of life without flinching.

THIRD SENIOR: It stands waiting, to show that we must always be ready to help people in their need.

FOURTH SENIOR: It stands unadorned to show us that we must be humble, for there is no one too mean to have its help.

FIFTH SENIOR: It stands immovable, to teach us to give without asking for reward or gratitude, for it helps equally the good and the bad, the thankful and the thankless.

SIXTH SENIOR: It stands continually, to teach us to be faithful and persevering in the common tasks of every day.

SEVENTH SENIOR: It is set in the center of the circle of fellowship, which stretches through the past and the future and goes out from Northwick to all India and beyond India to the circle of the whole world.

8. CROSS ON THE OPEN LOTUS

This fourth type seems to be the rarest; but the human heart may be trusted eventually to fashion fresh symbols as it becomes more proficient in the interpretation of thoughts and emotions that have come to be vividly real. The visioner of such true symbols is a benefactor of his people. For these first four types there is very little adverse criticism.

V. One will find, however, instances where a classical symbol from the West is associated with a classical symbol of some non-Christian religion. The cross superimposed on the open lotus flower has been freely used on the chapel furniture of the United Theological College of South India and Ceylon, Bangalore. This combination can be seen on each side of the altar front, on the reading desk, and most plainly on the two chancel chairs. (See No. 8.)

VI. Still more venturesome is the outright adoption of a classical symbol of some non-Christian religion with an attempted Christian reinterpretation of its meaning. An illustration of this type is found in the lotus capital carved on most of the fifty columns of the beautiful chapel of Trinity College (Church Missionary Society),

Kandy, Ceylon, which embodies many elements of Singhalese architecture. (See No. 9; also Nos. 28-33.) From the index it will be seen that the lotus appears in twenty-seven of our illustrations; and the cross superimposed on the lotus (type V) in fifteen.

Some of the criticisms of these last two types will be considered in Chapter IV.

As we think of the artisans of the younger churches, we may well recall how

Jehovah spake unto Moses, saying, See, I have called by name Bezalel . . . and I have filled him with the Spirit of God, in wisdom, and in understanding, and in knowledge, and in all manner of workmanship, to devise skilful works, to work in gold, and in silver, and in brass, and in cutting of stones for setting, and in carving of wood, to work in all manner of workmanship . . . . And in the hearts of all that are wise-hearted I have put wisdom, that they may make all that I have commanded thee. (*Exodus* 31:1-6.)

At this high level let artisans in the younger churches be spiritually approached—the carvers of wood and stone, the weavers of fine cloth, and those who work in plaster or wall designs. Out of the texture of their experience, retaining all that is good in their own culture and supplementing it from the rich Western store, will come fresh "glory and honor" from all nations to be brought into the city of God. The increasing spiritual maturity of the younger churches awakens expectancy throughout the ecumenical church that they can bring meaningful forms of expression of their own to the Church Universal.

9

9. THE LOTUS

II : Some Spiritual Values in "Things Visible"

There is a silent ministry of outward things and actions that have an inner meaning. When a thing is made or done, not with the aim of producing resemblance to something but rather of suggesting an affinity or spiritual relationship to what is not shown, it is called a symbol. As used here a symbol means something presented to the senses that stands for and reminds us of something else. It is an outward and visible sign of an inner and spiritual reality.

The word "prayer" is such a symbol. It does not itself resemble that inner state when the whole being turns toward God; but when we learn the English language, it becomes a recognized symbol for that state. Similarly, the touching picture of the little Indian girls (No. 10) does not resemble prayer, but we have learned to interpret that posture and reverent attitude as standing for a certain inner state. If one's aim is to produce a photograph of these children, then the picture is merely a mechanical reproduction. But if this picture is used to invest outward posture with an inner meaning, it then becomes a symbol. Just as a madonna is not merely a portrait of an artist's model and a baby, so this picture need not be merely a photograph of a particular event. It may take on a universal significance, pointing toward a living experience.

It is easy to catch the larger inner "significance" (literally, that to which a "sign" is "made") of the kneeling Indian girls, for we are familiar with the spiritual attitude associated with that posture. It takes more instruction for the uninitiated to catch the religious meanings associated with the lamb, dove, pelican or anchor; or with the lotus, dragon or cherry blossom. The degree of approximation of form and idea may vary; but with symbols there is always an inner picture for which the outer representation was made.

The Bible is constantly using the material and tangible to stimulate us to grasp some great insight. Numerous symbolic actions were employed by the Hebrew prophets as a means of attracting attention and impressing their teachings upon their hearers—Samuel's robe

10

accidentally torn by Saul, Ahijah's garment divided into twelve pieces, the horns worn by Zedekiah, the broken staff of Zechariah, Isaiah walking barefoot for three years, Jeremiah's shattered earthen vessel and linen girdle hidden in a rock, Ezekiel's shaved head and the removal of all his household goods. A much more inclusive list

10. PRAYER

could be made. Our Lord's teaching was generally clothed in figurative and symbolic form—the pearl of great price, the lost and wandering sheep, the working leaven, the house founded upon a rock, the sower of the seed, the laborers in the vineyard, the unjust judge, and the beautiful story of the prodigal son. Parables are symbols—stories pointing beyond themselves.

There were mountains around Jerusalem; but the psalmist would have them be more than mountains — they should symbolize how Jehovah is round about his people. The visible is constantly used to suggest the invisible — "as a grain of mustard seed," "as a hen gathereth her chickens," "as the tares are gathered," "as the lightning cometh," "as a thief in the night," "as a branch cannot bear fruit of

11

itself," "as a father," "as good stewards," "as we have many members," "as the body is one," "as new-born babes"—where shall we stop? We call these likenesses similes, but we might just as well speak of the objects involved as symbols.

The range of "things that are made" that may help reveal the "invisible things" of the spirit is of manifold variety. Symbols are found in form, language, action, number and color; in things verbal, visual and dramatic; in sounds from words, music and bells; in rituals, ceremonies and all the plastic arts. In historic theology, creeds and confessions are treated under the heading, "Symbolics." It would seem that the need of all kinds of symbolism is inwoven in human nature. However, this volume is limited predominantly to those suggestions of the intangible and the spiritual that can be visibly reproduced in the pages of a book.

Symbols have been useful in various ways. In the early centuries of the church, where Christians found refuge from repressive forces in the catacombs, pictorial expressions of their faith had to be in disguised forms, veiled under types and figures that would not arouse suspicion. The fish became a symbol for the Saviour, because the Greek word for fish is an acrostic from the Greek phrase meaning, "Jesus Christ, Son of God, Saviour." Our Lord was depicted as the legendary Orpheus with his lyre; or as a Good Shepherd, since the god Hermes, with a sheep across his shoulder, was a common figure in that day. The palm of victory and anchor of hope were familiar enough as emblems among contemporary non-Christians to excite no particular suspicion. Thus symbols had an early Christian use in disguising one's connection with a persecuted group.

Furthermore, there are aspects of experience and reality that, at their best, can be apprehended only "as in a glass darkly." Since it is not easy to impart certain spiritual insights in words, artists and builders of churches have devised pictorial metaphors that suggest a wealth of spiritual meaning. Eternity is suggested by a circle; the Trinity, by a triangle; the atonement, by a pelican plucking open her breast and feeding her young with her own blood. Just as we resort to ceremonies, liturgies and music to aid expression, so symbols help us with many an abstract conception.

A third function of symbolism is as a factor in education. Those who teach truth in its mere abstractness will scarcely influence the

12

popular mind. Truth, therefore, needs certain concrete aids in order to make itself at home in many minds. From this point of view symbols have to do with knowledge, and apart from that knowledge their value is largely lost. They are intended to say something, to be communicative, to inform.

Before the art of writing had been developed, man not only supplemented the audible word with the visible gesture, but used some pictorial representation to impress men's minds. And later, when books were still the rare and costly possessions of the privileged because printing had not as yet been invented, walls and windows were used to embody the Christian message. This use of Christian symbolism flowered forth at its maximum in medieval Europe. We read much of church walls forming the Bible of the Poor, and of priests leading bands of pilgrims to some stained-glass window to explain a biblical theme or to recount the heroism of some saint. Heaven was pictured with its meadows "white and green and red"; but even more determinative for that age were the somber, clear-cut figures of demons and the tortures of hell.

By the thirteenth century man had come to believe that God intended every created thing to be a symbol of his purposes, and hence churches built by man to his glory could be no less eloquent. Almost every stone or feature of a cathedral had or was given its symbolic meaning—three portals stood for the Trinity; double doorways, for the two natures of our Lord; a church resting on twelve pillars recalled the twelve apostles; a bell rope stood for humility because it hung downward. This result came partly through the conscious use of well-known symbolism, but also as the result of interpretations of what originally were free, artistic impulses following their own bent.

Thus we find the mind of the Middle Ages bodied forth in sculpture and in glass, or wrought out in wood, in beaten metal, or in rich tapestry. Their craftsmen were poets. Religion was a passion and produced its wealth of skillfully fabricated symbolism and of carved, painted or embroidered scenes from Bible or church history. Representative art, along with literature, formed part of the ways of knowing God. This art was charged with meaning — its function was mediatory. It is true that this medieval symbolism had its dangerous aspects, some of which will be mentioned in a later chapter. But the

13

underlying supposition was that avenues to the soul need not be limited to the ear or to the printed page.

But let us not think that symbolism has been confined to medieval Europe. True, majestic Rheims has during the seven hundred years of its history accumulated an endless wealth of symbolism carved upon its glorious west front or pictured in its splendid stained glass. But the contemporary mind is inclined to ask what that means today to designers of churches in America, in India, in China, and in the isles of the sea. One answer is found across the street from where I write. There stands Riverside Church, where great sermons are preached by word of mouth, and where sculptured stone, carved wood and stained glass add their silent but manifold and impressive messages. As a background for considering meaningful decoration in the younger churches a digression may be made at this point that we may see what this modern church in the city of New York has done.

Over the main entrance of Riverside Church the figure of the Christ (No. 11) looks out above the traffic of the city's streets, surrounded by the traditional symbols of the four evangelists—the angel, lion, bull and eagle. It is as though the Christ of the Gospels were saying to a modern city, "Oh, Jerusalem, Jerusalem, how often would I . . . but ye would not."

But this modern city is vastly different from the old Jerusalem. The world upon which the Christ looks out today has been greatly influenced and vastly changed by science, philosophy and religion. Hence each of the three inner rings of the upper archway contains fourteen figures representing the fourteen leading persons in these three respective fields. The arch of science begins with Hippocrates, Euclid and Archimedes, and ends with Pasteur, Lister and Einstein. The arch of philosophy begins with Pythagoras, Socrates and Plato, and ends with Kant, Hegel and Emerson. At one end of the arch of religion are Moses, Confucius, Buddha and Mohammed, while at the more modern end are Luther, Calvin, Bunyan, Carey and Livingstone. The first and fifth rings, flanking those just described, are devoted entirely to the figures of angels (literally "messengers"), reminders of hidden but ever present possibilities of spiritual reinforcement, which is the incalculable part of all progress.

Immediately below the seated figure of the Christ a narrow wavy

14

11. ENTRANCE, RIVERSIDE CHURCH, NEW YORK

line runs completely across the design—a conventional "cloud band" to suggest the elevation of the Christ above the immediate surroundings. Below this cloud band, three panels picture the struggle between good and evil in the members of a household. In the center the father stands behind the family table. To his left, members move off toward self-indulgence; to his right, better elements are triumphing. The lowest panel above the two doors includes the twelve apostles.

Lowest of the figures are five at the left of the doors— Isaiah, Jeremiah, Hosea, Amos and Micah; and five at the right—the saints Simeon, Stephen, Paul, Barnabas and Timothy. Thus symbolically there surround the congregation, as it enters and leaves the building, the men who stood for prophecy in the Old Testament and for the rich Christian fellowship of the New.

Inside the church, sculptured, carved or painted representations abound on every hand. More than two hundred subjects are found in the stained-glass windows; more than forty themes from the rich imagery of the *Book of Jeremiah* are found on the carved capitals of the pillars in the nave. The seven panels of the chancel screen portray the seven outstanding characteristics of our Lord's life and ministry, and contain ninety statues. The most prominent figure in each panel is that of our Lord, and about him are the great souls of the past who have faithfully carried out his teachings and example. The panel for Christ as Teacher contains Aquinas, Drummond, Arnold, Erasmus and Pestalozzi. Among the eighteen figures in the panel representing the Christ "who went about doing good" are St. Francis of Assisi, Ann Judson, Lincoln, General Armstrong, Florence Nightingale and William Booth. The missionaries' panel shows John Eliot, St. Augustine, Francis Xavier, Morrison and Judson, among others. And so on, with Christ as the Good Physician, the Prophet, the Reformer and the Lover of Beauty.

The question was raised as to why such a modern church should express itself in a way that some associate only with medieval cathedrals. One definite answer is indicated by a small, thirty-one page pamphlet composed by the children of the third grade in Riverside's church school. In the preface they say, "We have been explaining the different arts of our church. All the interesting things we have found out we have put into a guide for children who visit Riverside Church." They describe the Builder's Window, with Jesus

16

as a boy in his father's workshop in the center, and around this picture representations of lumbermen bringing in huge logs, diggers of the foundation, bricklayers, the architect. The Bible Window attracts their attention, for it was the children of the church who gave an idea for this window. They wanted the words "God is love" in all languages because God loves everyone. Symbolic pictures suggest that parts of the Bible were once passed on as songs; later, but before paper was invented, messages were carved on stone; then came the printing press, so that the valued book need no longer be chained to the pulpit, and all might read.

The Children's Window, also, was planned as a project by the children of the church in preparation for the present building. It pictures boys and girls from many lands—China, Czechoslovakia, Africa and India. The Jewish boy—Jesus—is in the center. Sometimes they call it their "World Friendship Window."

The Music Window shows men in Africa and American Indians beating on drums; men in ancient China striking metals hung on a rod; the first harp made in Egypt; Orpheus with his lyre; David playing before Saul; instruments from Assyria; and, among others, the phonograph, radio, and, at the top of the window, a large church organ.

Among other things they give a page to the chancel screen, described above. Do you not like the way these children caught its message? "The world needs doctors and teachers. It needs reformers and prophets. It needs people who know how to be friends. And so they set up statues of men and women who have done such work in the world."

There is an increasing demand in the West that church decorations should mean something, that esthetic surfaces should have content and not be ends in themselves, that mere prettiness be avoided. One large Western church believes enough in the educative values of properly designed stained-glass windows to grade the content of windows in each room of its church school to the age-group that meets there regularly. A similar appreciation of the educational value of symbols can be found in many centers in the East, as the descriptions in Part II show. But if this educative end is to be attained, attention must be given to developing literacy in artistic language as well as in the written word. Especially should children be taught the meanings embodied by their church in fresco, glass or carving. It may take years of teaching—even a second generation—before representations come to have their full Christian meaning. In more than one instance, search of official records failed to reveal the meaning of some shields, altar designs, or coats of arms, so that the local correspondent had to give his individual interpretation. Manifestly, in such cases the symbol is not a live factor in religious education.

A fourth use of symbolism is to express the religious continuity of the present with the past. This was a conscious purpose motivating the range of subjects sculptured in the richly adorned chapel at the University of Chicago, dedicated in 1928, where among other things the march of religion through the centuries is embodied. The official guide books says that

the sculpture is . . . primarily symbolic in character. It seeks to set forth the religious continuity of the present with the past. . . . The sculpture would say to the observer, "We are a continuous part of the great heroic religious development of mankind." . . . The whole sculptured front thus comes to possess a dramatic unity, the heroes and molders of religion marching across the stage of history . . . and reminding us of our own religious continuity with the past and hence also with the future.

Thus the inclusion of symbols almost unchanged from early or medieval representations, along with the increasing trend to draw subjects from modern or even contemporary life, may serve to remind us of the unbroken stream of Christian life that flows down through the centuries.

Still another use of symbolism is to suggest ideas for contemplation as one enters a church or awaits the beginning of the service. The physical work of art may invite the observer to a spiritual act of his own. We can almost hear some of the symbols saying, "Reflect on this fact or on this truth." A Chinese, when asked why he attached a cross to his watch chain, replied, "I like to put my hand in my pocket and be reminded of a great sacrifice." An altar candle to some may be merely a source of light; but a congregation might learn to say, with Abbie Graham, "As I watch the Christmas candles burn I see in them a symbol of the Great Love which dipped a lustrous spirit into a human form that the world in its darkness might be illumined and made beautiful."

18

It was, in part, this use of symbolism that lay back of the sculptural scheme of the chapel of the University of Chicago. The official interpretation points out that

for the casual passerby, it contributes variety and lights and shadows to the general effect. The closer observer who stops to ask who these figures are will find a meaning in each of them; while together, . . . even before he enters the building, they will strike for him the note of praise.

The writer goes so far as to say that the chapel would be worth while even if no service were to be held in it and no use ever made of it; for, amid the great quadrangles of the university, the note of nobility and beauty struck by this dominant building symbolizes for each student generation spiritual values and immaterial ideals.

No one believes so much in the "direct approach" to God that he would deny to the wayfarer supports along the way. Only the most mature and disciplined natures can engage in worship of a purely spiritual type without any ceremonies, parables or symbols. But if spiritual meditation, thus induced, is to be effective, worshippers must not expect the art forms themselves to accomplish the work within; they are meant merely to start a process that must be carried on by the worshipper himself. From this standpoint all depends upon what the observer does with the symbol. What is expected of him is an act of contemplation. To use only the eyes in looking at a symbol is just as bad as to engage only the ear in hearing a sermon; in each case there should be something more than an "artistic" performance. Thus the religious symbol at its best is conceived, not merely as a new form of material beauty, but as a means of creating new persons. However, if in this way a symbol is to become dynamic, its deeper meaning and its history should become common property.

One reason why the crest of the United Missionary Girls' School in Calcutta (No. 12) has been so effective in stimulating school spirit is that pupils thoroughly understand the symbols and had a part in choosing them. For two years the girls of this school had been feeling after a suitable school crest; in 1930 they adopted the emblems of the sun and the lotus—the sun standing for light, knowledge, wisdom; and the lotus standing for purity. As the lotus blooms in the sunlight, so these girls wish to grow in the light of knowledge, and freely give to others as the lotus gives its sweet scent without any price. One

19

12. THE SUN AND THE LOTUS

student, looking at the crest, prayed, "O God, give us the purity of the lotus, so that we may give up all evil thoughts. We are blind travelers in the dark way of our life, so kindly hold thy burning candle in front of us, and guide us in thine own way." Similarly, if we turn back to "Christ, the Burden Bearer" (No. 7) we will be impressed with the conscious preparation taken to make the school badge a potential factor in meditation.

Consider further the beautiful grapevine design shown in No. 13. Like most symbols this vine cannot be judged by verisimilitude; its value does not lie in its resemblance to any natural species. The real picture that is intended is not in the carved design, but in the mind of Him who said:

I am the true vine . . . . As the branch cannot bear fruit of itself except it abide in the vine; so neither can ye, except ye abide in me. I am the vine, ye are the branches: he that abideth in me, and I in him, the same beareth much fruit: for apart from me ye can do nothing. (*John* 15 :1, 4-5.)

That is the picture that must be re-enacted in the mind of the observer; the carving points the way to a possible realization in consciousness. We may recognize, therefore, that art forms can be signposts inviting worshippers to an inward act. The problem is whether any particular representation is appropriate and effective.

20

13. PEIPING UNION BIBLE TRAINING SCHOOL. Besides the cross on the altar there are three crosses in the pierced grapevine carving, one at each end and one in the center, all unlike. Each of the simple benches has a cross carved on its upright end. The exterior of this chapel has two rows of small round beam ends under the roof; on one row is painted the lotus, and about twenty designs of crusaders' crosses on the other row. The very location of the chapel is symbolic, for it comes first within the entrance and therefore in the most honored place, and its position between the dormitory and the classrooms is intended to suggest that it should be the center of life

21

Much is done in the younger churches to instruct the understanding; not enough to stir the imagination and to develop the emotions. Modern psychology is showing that human behavior is influenced not alone by ideas, but by that which appeals to the unconscious and subconscious. The strong feeling that a symbol may awaken, even when its intellectual content is not explicitly in mind, has not been fully appreciated. We may well ask with the Reverend H. P. Thompson, "Are we in danger of thinking too much of giving a simple setting to the worship of simple people, and too little of what they may rise to, when a greater setting gives full rein to the capacity that is in them?" The exercises of worship do not, of course, absolutely require the aid of art and architecture any more than they require the help of music and of eloquence. But no one would wish that worship should always be attended by cheap music and mean surroundings. Possibly it may be agreed that the Puritan reaction, which made a virtue of bleak, prosaic severity, was carried to an extreme in the West and need not be reproduced in Asia and Africa.

Whether artistic representations function in these five ways depends not alone upon whether some skilled artificer has enriched arch or wall or altar in our churches, or has thoughtfully designed the seal or crest of school and diocese. Significance must be restored to forms that for many have become mere ornaments—and, as has been noted, "significance" means literally that toward which a sign is made. As one sits in the chapel of the Woman's Christian College, Tokyo, how is one to gain support for meditation from the altar's three symbols (No. 139), if one has not been helped to read their meaning—"From weakness, through the resurrection, to victory"? The meaningful Kimwha church (No. 158), or the crest of the *gurukul* at Madras (No. 67), may "signify" little unless someone takes the trouble, possibly beginning with youth, to interpret the artist's work. To rest content with the decorative value of an age-old symbol is what is called estheticism. One might as well be satisfied for a congregation to be entranced with the pleasurable sound of the church bell without teaching them that this "signifies" or points toward the oncoming service of worship.

Many of the representative forms shown in this book have been so voided of meaning that it has taken repeated inquiries from those most closely connected with them to discover what thoughts they were intended to suggest. A bursting pomegranate pictured on the communion table abides as a mere adornment unless the congregation is reminded by it of our Lord, who was able to burst the tomb on Easter Day and came forth alive; or see in it a type of the resurrection of all true believers in Jesus Christ. When, however, art forms in church decoration do enter into the religious education of the church, the thought of a congregation may be directed in ways that may become a constant source of spiritual experience.

How can such meaningful art forms be created? Ordinarily the process of developing symbols with vital religious suggestions is a gradual one. If they cannot be imposed suddenly from without, neither are they created until new ideas and ideals are believed strongly and felt deeply. They will have greatest significance when in each land its artistic genius, informed and inspired by the truths and purposes of Christianity, is enlisted for the church, and when its Christian artisans are loyal to the Craftsman's Creed:

I hold with none who think not work a boon vouchsafed to man that he may aid his kind with offerings from his chisel, wheel, or loom, fashioned with loving heart and loving mind. All of the fine traditions and the skill, come from my elders through the long line down, are mine to use to raise our craft's renown and mine to teach again with reverent will. Thus do I live to serve, though least for pay, with fingers which are masters of the tool and eyes which light to see the pattern's play as it unfolds, obedient to each rule of our dear art. So all my craft is praise to God — at once part homage and part song. My work's my prayer, I sing the whole day long as faith and beauty shape the forms I raise.

III : Symbols and the Ecumenical Mind

Certain adjustments in thought and judgment are necessary if we are really to appreciate the richness in diversity in the ecumenical church. We should not allow ourselves to be incapable, still less unwilling, to recognize meaning or beauty in unfamiliar 'forms. It may easily be that a given bit of artistry may seem capricious or even distasteful. Yet, if we are convinced that it expresses the intelligible and reasonable tastes, interests and aspirations of those who originally produced it, that distaste can change into appreciation based on understanding.

We must be flexible in the meanings attached to any given symbol. Take, for example, the matter of liturgical colors. The artists of the Renaissance developed a symbolism of color that was valid for that age and that is meaningful for those who know the key.

In this symbolism, white stood for purity, joy and life; but in China, white is invariably the color of mourning. Black, in the West, generally stands for death, darkness, despair, sorrow; but in India, the faces of the gods Krishna and Rama are blue-black with "divine blackness." Most colors are polar—they can be used in a good or a bad sense—and hence, in the West, red can stand for ardent love and a burning zeal for the faith, or for cruelty and blood-guiltiness; but for the Chinese, red stands for festivity. The ribbons in the Bible resting on many a Western lectern are changed to purple for the days of Lent; but purple has no penitential significance in Eastern Asia. Clerical gowns in the West are black, while saffron robes are worn by holy men in India.

If the ecumenical church is to have a uniform sequence of liturgical colors, should the choice and sequence of color be imposed from a single culture? Or is this one field in which there can be variety in the Church Universal?

It is not alone in color symbolism that cultural differences exist. There are difficulties in taking over wholesale the religious iconography of the West. For China, the dove is an emblem of long life; the symbol would have to be retaught to stand for the Holy Spirit. For that country, also, the lamb is the symbol of filial piety since it kneels respectfully when taking its mother's milk; should one risk introducing it for the Lamb of God? The dragon, in the West, represents temptation and the evil one—something to be vanquished by St. Michael or St. George. However, "the Eastern dragon is not the gruesome monster of medieval imagination, but the genius of strength and goodness. He is the spirit of change, therefore of life itself." In the West, the censer and smoking incense have from the earliest days been the symbol of prayer, which ascends heavenward as a sweet-smelling savor. To the Shinranists of Japan, and in fact to all Buddhists, incense is a symbol of the truth of impermanency—for all life to them is as fleeting as rising smoke.

Again, a Western artist will represent the annunciation by means of a lily and a dove; the Indian will probably use the lotus and the white swan. The Tree of Life will appear as the apple in Dante's Italy, the sycamore in Egypt, the ash in Scandinavia, and the ásvattha in India. As we have already seen, the fish early became a symbol for our Lord. But when even Westerners find it hard to remember this acrostic, and since China has no alphabet, would it be worth while to introduce this symbol to China? There is the additional difficulty that for them the fish is an emblem of wealth, abundance and regeneration (because of the similarity in pronunciation of the words for "fish" and for "superfluity").

The matter of regional or geographic climate should not be overlooked in the aspiration for an ecumenical mind. When Christendom was as yet confined to the domain of Western "Christian" civilization, the symbolic suggestions from Europe's various seasons were built into the Church Year. For example, Easter fittingly came when in Europe all nature was springing into new life. But listen to the pleading words of Francis Xavier writing in 1543 from Goa, on the southwest coast of India, to Ignatius of Loyola, the Father Master of the Jesuit Order:

In these countries nature has so completely inverted the regular order of the seasons, that when on the other coast of India it is full summer, here on this side we are feeling the winter; and so on this, when they are under the winter colds, we are burnt up by the summer heats. And the heat in summer is something incredible. The sun is so hot, that fish begin to rot as soon as they die.

The Governor has charged me to lay all these facts carefully before you, and to beg of you in the name of God, and if such a thing be possible, you will get the Pope to change the time of Lent in these parts to the months of June and July, at which time of year the heat begins to relent, and there is much less navigation, on account of the roughness of the sea.

So the milder temperature would make it easy for most people to fast, and the return of Lent at that time would be a sort of reminder, and they would then easily obey the precepts of the Church as to confession and communion. This measure is one which seems of the greatest importance for the service of God, unless you see any objection to it. The Governor entreats you earnestly not to let anything that can be done in this matter be left unattempted through any want of exertion on the part of his advocate. You will be rewarded for your trouble by the gratitude of all inhabitants of these countries, and you will have a share in the fruits of the divine worship and the merits which will be acquired in consequence of all those graces. Adieu.

Manifestly Xavier was not finding symbolic reinforcement from India's climate for Europe's Church Year.

An interesting adjustment in ecclesiastical regulations due to varying geographical conditions was made by Pope Nicholas IV in 1289. At that time it was a universal rule that no caps should be worn by priests during services of worship as a symbol of reverence. But the monks of Kelso, Scotland, represented to the Pope that they were *"in frigida zona regionis Scotiae";* and those of Lindores (also in Scotland) pleaded that some of them had suffered frequent and protracted illness from having their heads uncovered in the unheated churches of Scotland's cold climate — some even had died from exposure. Hence, the Pope granted permission for them to wear caps during the service of great festivals and in procession.

On the whole, however, there are relatively few petitions for changes in the Church Year to conform to the symbolic appropriateness of the local season. No doubt in an ecumenical church, Advent, Christmastide, Epiphany, the Lenten season, Easter and Ascension Day must be at uniform times around the world. But that should not blind us to the fact of their original correlation to the weather and to the seasonal work of Europe; and that in another hemisphere if the rains are on, or the crops must be watched, or harvest is at its height, the helpful sympathy of nature with the given celebration may be absent.

The ecumenical mind must take into consideration different psychological climates, also. We are used to the idea of such differences as we think back over the centuries. The medieval mind, for example, was mystic rather than factual. The scientific age had not yet come, separating cause and effect; hence imagination was less restrained, and analogy, allegory and hidden meanings had peculiar force in that day.

We do not, however, always plan with recognition of the fact that all the psychological differences of the centuries are present in today's cross section of humanity. In our world Christian community are people of high culture and also multitudes of poor, illiterate folk. Even in a single land the church may include scholars who depend on printed books and magazines, as well as backward tribes not unlike the primitives of another age.

Even sophisticated metropolitan churches, as we have seen, give a large place to symbolic representations. All the more do simple people need outward signs to express spiritual meanings. Abstract ideas are by them best assimilated through parable, analogy, allegory, ritual and symbol—after the usage prevalent in the infancy of the world's religious history. For simple people the appeal should not be mainly intellectual. From a Roman Catholic source, for example, comes the suggestion for a baptismal service that is filled with symbolism. The white robe should be worn as an emblem of innocence. A lighted candle stands for illumination of faith; the use of oil represents the abundance of grace. A blow upon the cheek suggests the warfare in which the resolute Christian is engaged. A turn is made to the West when renouncing all evil, and to the East in making profession of faith. All this is in accord with a truth enunciated by modern education as well as by an ancient Buddhist sutra—"Whatever is not adapted to such and such persons as are to be taught cannot be called a 'teaching.' "

Highly gifted and intellectual people, also, may differ in their cultural psychologies. It is well known, for example, that in general through the centuries India has not valued the historical. To her philosophers, Christianity appears obsessed with the historical point of view because Christianity bases its message and claims on history. All this tends to influence the art of the two cultures. In so far as

India conforms to its traditional emphasis, the mythical is preferred rather than the more naturalistic portraiture of the West.

Biblical symbols indigenous to Palestine and to the West may find no exact counterpart in other lands, as any translator of the Bible has experienced. Sins that become "white as snow" in one place may have to become "as the white of a coconut" in Ceylon. For the Ba-ila of Central Africa, who have never seen snow, the impression of great whiteness comes from a cloud of egrets that may be seen by them clustering upon a tree and glistening like a mound of snow in the light of the westering sun. For them, sins may become white as *lukobo* (egrets). For the Eskimo "the lamb of God" may have to be "the little seal of God." Sheep are unfamiliar in Japan; and hence a Japanese pastor, when asked what the bronze goat on the desk in his study meant, could reply, "It reminds me of my Saviour."

To appreciate in any adequate way the deeper and genuinely indigenous symbols created by the various members in the world-wide Christian community requires a passing beyond the provincial —a certain enlargement of the self. Eventually the ecumenical mind must make a distinction between the pleasure it takes in certain familiar colors, forms and designs in its own culture and the pleasure that can be taken in seeing other colors, forms and designs that congenially and adequately meet artistic needs in another culture. In other words, the ecumenical mind must make a distinction between individual taste and objective beauty. Moreover, we shall not catch the significance of symbols from another culture if we bring to them merely the superficial attention of the casual visitor to a museum. We must pass beyond the curious observation of the exterior to the intelligent apprehension of inner meanings. We have to lay aside our own preferences, find what the artist in some distant land is attempting to do, and reconstruct the environment in which he worked. It is to reinforce just this warning that Dr. Ananda K. Coomaraswamy, of the Fine Arts Museum, Boston, quotes Mencius as saying that to grasp the true meaning of words requires not so much a dictionary as a rectification of the personality. With similar import what Goethe said of pictures may well be said of symbols: "Who would understand the painter must go to the painter's land."

It is one thing to realize that the world Christian community is made up of a multitude out of every nation, of all tribes and peoples and tongues; it is another to sense the natural corollaries from that fact. For one thing, it means that each race will have its characteristic thoughts about God; each tongue will have its favorite metaphors; each people, its meaningful representations. Western Christian symbols, though older, are just as national as are Asian or African forms, and should not naïvely be assumed to be ordained for universal use. The older Christendom will undoubtedly share its rich store of symbols with the larger community attained by the expansion of the faith. But the older churches must none the less be ready to understand and to appreciate what is worthy in the artistry of lands to which their messengers have gone. In this mutuality of giving and receiving the Church Universal will be enriched.

IV : Precautions concerning "Things That Are Made"

That there are dangers in the use of symbolic representations would be admitted by all who have thoughtfully considered the question, whether in connection with the older or with the younger churches. Warnings mainly come from those concerned for the latter. Some of the distinctive dangers in each area will be given in the various introductory sections of Part II.

For one thing, material forms are fixed, and hence tend to conserve outworn conceptions. In some such way the continuance of medieval religion in many a twentieth-century church may have been helped by this persistence of archaic faiths and ideals impressively embodied in brick and mortar. Some of our historic art forms are outworn or stand for ideas that are not truly real to us. Western symbols, therefore, should not be uncritically inculcated in a younger church. Also, because these material forms are external, they invite imitation and repetition without fresh thought and life.

Again, all of us, unless we are spiritually awake, tend to see the sculptured or painted form, and not the particular state of mind that the symbol was meant to inspire. In a dull mood we are likely to miss the idea, the spirit, or the sentiment, and experience only the visible. There is a real danger, therefore, that for certain backward peoples the physically tangible symbol may take the place of the thing signified. In that case the symbol becomes a fetish or idol. From this point of view idolatry may be defined as the misuse of symbols. For example, an illiterate sudra, on entering a church in India and seeing an eagle with outspread wings (to Western Christians, a symbol of inspiration), bowed with clasped hands before it as a god. Because of this danger of idolatry even the use of the cross as a fixture in the place of worship has been a controversial question in some quarters of India.

The misunderstanding of symbols has not been unknown in the West. Medieval symbolism, especially, has its warnings for our day. The Biblia Pauperum of that day was a rough-and-ready book, with crudities and superstitions that art forms helped to fix in mind.

30

Often they tended to materialize the church's doctrines or to encourage ascribing human characteristics to God—defects likely to come from all popularizations. Metaphors may help the masses, but a good servant may become an unruly master.

A modern scholar, Dr. G. G. Coulton, tells us that medieval symbolism "was far less logical and systematic, far less consistent, and far less universal, than modern antiquaries imagine," and that even in that day men of deep piety, primarily concerned with the religion of their flocks, were conscious of harmful results from ill-formed sculptures which might cause derision, or from popular misconceptions of Christian doctrine, as when, for example, the Trinity would be represented by three solemn figures identical in their features. He quotes one who knew well the English parish life of a thousand years ago as sadly lamenting how the common folk of his day were apt to mistake even the ordinary ecclesiastical symbolism. "These four Evangelists be likened to four divers beasts; that is, for Mark a lion, for Matthew a man, for Luke a calf, and for John an eron (eagle). Wherefore, many lewd men ween that they were beasts and not men."

The remedy for this danger would seem to be definite and constructive religious education. A little Indian girl garlanded the new cross in her school chapel and left a clay lamp burning near it. To avoid a repetition of this the principal made it the practice at the beginning of each school year to explain that the cross is not an object of worship, but is a symbol reminding us of what Christ did for us, and of the loving sacrifice and service we must try to render to others. Garlanding and clay lamps were not allowed; but with this background of careful preparation the cross continued to have its place in creating a worshipful atmosphere and in stimulating meditation.

Since traditional meanings and values may linger on in a non-Christian symbol carrying a flavor of paganism, there are Christian nationals who do not wish to build or paint or symbolize in the vernacular. They do not wish to be reminded of the religion they have abandoned; they prefer to make a clean breach with their religious past, and hence do not resent the foreign character of their adopted faith.

A missionary in India whose last ten years have been largely given to experiments in indigenous architecture, especially in so far as it deals with local design and tradition, reports that he has spent

31

hours in fruitless search for suitable symbols; all too often those on temples deal with Hindu deities or with incidents in their lives.

An apparently innocent-looking bird or flower carved on a Hindu column has some connection with one of the gods and gives offence to Christians. Anything savoring of idolatry must be taboo. Hence converts are often fanatically opposed to the carving of the human figure; and this prevents substituting Christian saints for the carvings of Hindu deities.

This stress upon complete separation from anything that suggests an older faith probably makes apostasy to the former loyalties more difficult. Hence, any suggestion that Christians should adopt, or even adapt, non-Christian symbols has met with scant approval. An experienced associate of the Union Architectural Service in China reports:

The Christian groups I try to serve do not want native symbols. They say it suggests only idolatry and paganism, which they are done with forever. I have tried to point out that our Western forms mostly have pagan ancestors, but to little avail. The Christian groups say Western forms mean for them a new-found freedom in Christ. It is only when some foreign group has the final authority that any Chinese motifs have been used by us. However, with the strong rise of national patriotism and a certain renaissance of interest in things Chinese we may see some change in this state of affairs.

Another experienced missionary, this time from India, gives several reasons to explain the entire absence of Indian symbolism in Christian use so far as he has observed:

There are relatively few new church buildings; most were built before the present trend to incorporate Indian motifs. Having worshipped in these churches for generations, Christians, who are extremely conservative in these matters, have come to accept buildings without decoration as the correct type. Moreover, the same congregation may have converts from Hinduism as well as from Islam, and symbolism adapted from the religious past of one group would not be acceptable to the other. In one section of the country converts are constantly on their guard to see that no Hindu or Moslem representation is introduced.

But this alien appearance of Christianity, which proves so congenial and so helpful to those already Christian, may be an obstacle to the one who is still an inquirer. If, however, the newcomer finds that certain elements in his treasured cultural heritage have been adjudged worthy of a place in the worship of the faith he is considering, he may be favorably disposed toward that faith. Such a familiar symbol may encourage a passer-by to enter a church; or to assure him, once within, that his artistic language is understood. As the late Sadhu Sundar Singh said, "The water of life must be offered to India in an Indian cup."

While there is danger in using a form that has pagan significance, there is also danger of altogether overlooking the possible noble implications of a symbol, and hence failing to build it into the Christian heritage. Thus there may be a conflict between a design that will best edify Christians long accustomed to Western forms and that which will really draw a non-Christian to Christianity without undue offense to his cultural loyalty—a conflict between Christian nurture of members and the evangelization of non-members. This dilemma suggests that for some weak Christian communities a policy of breaking with the past may be advisable at an early stage; but that when that community finds itself strongly grounded in the Christian faith, it could safely assimilate worthy aspects of the older cult without fear of harmful syncretism. Leaders develop with enough insight, experience and technique to use elements from the old heritage with discrimination and understanding. In either case, the question of the kind of artistic expression that the Christian movement makes is seen to have an importance of its own.

Many have doubts as to whether entrenched symbolism can ever be reinterpreted or divorced from its ancient associations. Here history has something to say. We have to remember that many Christian forms were taken over from Judaism, and that many of the religious symbols of the ancient Hebrews were in turn derived from the polytheistic religions of their neighbors. In the successive transfers, however, the fire of purification is manifest. Our Easter had pagan associations; nevertheless, it has become for us one of the most spiritual and soul-inspiring days of the Christian year. More sweepingly the *Catholic Encyclopedia* can say:

In the matter of baptisms and washings, of genuflections and other acts of reverence, of lights and sweet-smelling incense, of flowers and white vestures, of unction and the imposing of hands, of sacrifice and the rite of the communion banquet, the church has borrowed without hesitation from the common stock of significant actions known to all periods and to all nations.

33

In fact, history clearly shows that as Christianity went out into the Western world it took to itself national, racial and cultural modes of expression, and that without such adaptation it nowhere exists in the West. To remove symbols entirely from their traditional context and values may be difficult; but it is worth while seriously to consider whether it is not easier to habituate new meanings for old symbols than to introduce new symbols.

Few, perhaps, would object to the use of symbols of non-Christian religions in suggesting the march of religion across the centuries. This is just the purpose intended in a series of sculptures on the chapel of the University of Chicago. There is Zoroaster, reformer of the Persian faith, whose teachings affected later Judaism. Plato, as a molder of Greek religious thought, which was afterward to blend with Christianity, has a shield that bears the portico of a Greek temple supported by wings, since philosophy, to the Greek mind, gave wings to the soul. Ideal figures reveal the artist with the winged horse, the philosopher with the staff, the statesman with the scroll and the rods of office, and the scientist with the crystal and the open scroll—all conceived as buttressing true religion, in the broadest and highest sense.

Similarly, in the stained-glass window of Riverside Church, New York, devoted to the "International Character of Religion," among the fifteen pictures suggesting experiences in which religion has shown its disregard for national and racial boundaries we find, along with Jonah setting out for Nineveh and the Wise Men from the East, representations of Buddhism, Islam, Confucius and his disciples, and Lao-tse presenting his writings to the keeper of the gate.

In order to symbolize the variety in cultural heritage among the members of the Church of the Crossroads, Honolulu, carvings representing four great religious traditions were placed in the chancel, one at the foot on each side of the reading desk, and on each side of the pulpit (No. 14). The *Bo*-tree is used as a symbol of Buddhism (No. 15). For Zoroastrianism, since Light is the force fighting against Darkness, a flame-aureole is wrought into the design (No. 16). The religion of the Old Testament is symbolized by the multiple praying hands and by the face averted in adoring reverence— here the female face balancing the male (No. 17); while the pure white lotus represents Hinduism (No. 18).

34

14. CHANCEL, CHURCH OF THE CROSSROADS, HONOLULU

15. BUDDHISM

16. ZOROASTRIANISM

17. JUDAISM

18. HINDUISM

Certainly it is a dangerous thing for Westerner or national to urge upon a younger church some symbol from an older faith on the basis of a mere superficial and sentimental understanding of that symbol. The uncritical adoption of local motifs is as bad, on the one hand, as, on the other, is the assumption that Western forms are the unquestioned norm for all lands. Before adoption, non-Christian symbols should be known in their total significance; and this may require profound study, reconstructing the whole thought-world of the time and people that produced them. Just as an understanding of medieval art demands an appreciation of the spirit of the Middle Ages and the spirit of Christianity itself, so the language of non-Christian symbols has to be learned and not merely our superficial reaction to them noted.

For example, consider the lotus with Dr. Ananda K. Coomaraswamy, the well-known authority on Indian art. Long before Buddhism, Hindus used the many-petaled spread of the lotus to symbolize spatial expansion—the petals of the flowers being the points of the compass. From this it gets a cosmic significance as space wherein there can be any manifestation, or as that whereon all existence both is supported and passes away. The lotus was connected with the sun, since the moment of its opening corresponds with the dawn. To many Hindus it signifies the foot of God touching the earth. The lotus fittingly rests upon the waters—the primary metaphysical symbol of potentiality and universal supply.

Later, this ancient symbolism was taken up by Buddhism, and Buddha was universally represented as standing or sitting on the lotus. How superficial for one to think of this as an odd artistic fancy —putting him on a frail even if beautiful flower from which he might any time fall off into the water! Rather, this symbolism was saying to all who had learned the "language" that Buddha is on the platform of existence—for "he who stands or sits upon the lotus, 'lives.' " His foot touches naught of local earth, as much as to say that "all cosmic and not merely some or all terrestrial possibilities are at his command." Less essentially, the many petals, like spokes, suggest to Buddhists the Wheel of the Law. The expanded flower resting upon the surface of the placid waters typifies Nirvana—the ultimate repose of the soul after all desire has fled.

In the light of these traditional meanings associated with the

36

lotus, it is interesting to note that one of the adaptations of the lotus symbolism most frequently made by Christians is the cross surmounting the lotus. On the pillars or archways of many a church of indigenous architecture is to be found the cross sculptured above a lotus. This may be done with full appreciation of the metaphysical meanings as given in the texts of Hinduism and Buddhism and with a thoroughly considered judgment of how many of these older and traditional values should be taken over by Christians in the use of this new combination. Popularly, this Christian design is often taken to indicate that Christianity is the "fulfillment" of Buddhism; but manifestly such an interpretation sets aside all the traditional meanings.

There are, of course, more popular and familiar significances associated with the lotus. Professor Masaharu Anesaki, in his *Buddhist Art,* says that when Buddha attained enlightenment under the *Bo*-tree, compassion for his fellow-beings took possession of his mind. He saw them, as it is told, like lotus stems and buds in a lake, some immersed in the mud, others coming out of it or just appearing above the water, and still others beginning to blossom. Seeing this he determined to bring them all to full bloom and to the bearing of fruit. In other words, he became convinced of the possibility of extending the communion of Truth-winners to all sentient beings, who should in turn become Truth-winners.

There are still other more or less obvious analogies. The lotus is the symbol of purity and perfection because it grows out of the mud but is not defiled. As the open flower quietly rests upon the water facing the sun, the lotus could not help but stand for meditation. We, like the lotus, should bloom in response to the Light of Heaven (the Sun). In full bloom it pictures an awakened heart. Just as the lotus has its roots caught in the quagmire and its stem immersed in muddy water, and yet the flower rises above all this to exquisite beauty and purity, so we are to rise above all passion and selfish gain. Growing thus in the mud, it betrays no trace of its origin. Neither its flower nor its leaf is made wet by the water on which it rests; so we should live in the world, but be not of it.

With such a wealth of metaphysical as well as of popular symbolism, it is not strange that Christians have quite widely adopted the lotus. The index to this volume shows how extensively it has entered into Christian usage. It is found all the way from the Church of Al Mu Allakah in Egypt—one of the oldest existing places of Christian worship in the world, where a conventional lotus pattern is the main design—to Dr. Karl Ludwig Reichelt's Christian monastery near Hongkong (No. 86). In the West the rose is a common symbol for the Virgin Mary; it is not strange that one frequently finds the lotus associated with a madonna in an Eastern picture (see No. 117).

In the Hume Memorial Church in Ahmednagar, erected under the auspices of the American Congregational mission, there is a lotus flower window in pink and green, as a symbol for India, behind the pulpit; around the gallery in carved wood runs a lotus design; and again one finds the lotus on the chairs and sacramental table and about the base of the Indian dome towering high above the city. Thus the beautiful outline of the lotus reappears in all the decoration, speaking of its welcome to the Oriental sense of beauty. Nowhere in this church are there Western ecclesiastical symbols, nor any human or animal figure that might suggest idol worship.

Any Christian poet, moreover, who outstandingly wins the heart of his people will doubtless use the imagery of his own land and sing in the tongue of his own race. And so we find the great Christian Marathi poet, Narayan Vaman Tilak, making his tribute to our Lord in words that carry emotion to an Indian:

A living garland I entwine,
And offer at thy lotus feet.

It is possible that for Christians, in some cases, the sculptured and painted lotus on Christian churches means no more than a decorative embellishment congenial to those of a certain environment. But where its use is genuinely and thoughtfully symbolic, it would be interesting to know in each case what ideas Christian leaders would like to have stimulated in their congregations or in chance visitors by this particular representation. Just what, actually, is its content for religious education in these cases?

Another consideration is that in the choice of suitable acts and objects for religious symbolism, even if we were starting out deliberately to invent a ritual or decoration for church wall, it would be hard to avoid the charge of imitation of non-Christian symbols. Dr.

38

Coomaraswamy writes that "there are no symbols private to any religion. If, as an historian of art, I were asked to point to a specifically Christian or specifically Buddhist symbol, for example, I should be hard put to it to find an answer."

Consider the swastika, the inclusion of which in Christian art (see index) may jar on some. This is a symbol of great antiquity known to many peoples. It is found in remains of the bronze age; on the pottery of the early American Indians; and it is still woven into blankets by their descendants today. Scandinavian inscriptions show the swastika on the battle-ax of Thor. It was the monogram of Vishnu and Siva in India; and the Buddhists introduced it into China and Japan. It appears on the crowns of Lama deities in Tibet. It has been found depicted on the tombs at Hissarlik, the site of ancient Troy, in Etruscan cemeteries, on coins of Gaza and Corinth, on rock carvings in Sweden, and on Celtic stones in Britain.

Some hold it to be the earliest form of what later evolved into the cross. In standard Christian use the swastika is found as the "Rebated Cross," or as the "Cross Cramponnee." The swastika is fairly common on early Christian remains in Rome, probably indicating by this no relation of Christianity to the religions of Persia, Judea and Asia generally, but being the device by which the persecuted could at once portray and conceal the cross of their Lord. It is found, also, on many of the bronze and brass Christian crosses unearthed in North China. The name comes from the Sanskrit word meaning "to be," denoting resignation of spirit. But, in general, its meaning is obscure. Some hold it symbolizes the whirling movement when fire is made from turning a stick inserted in wood, and hence its use as a symbol of the sun's daily rotation. An old Chinese writer considers it a lucky sign "possessing ten thousand efficacies." It was used as a mark of benediction, of good omen and of health.

Similarly the lotus, surcharged with symbolism, has been loved as a sacred flower in many lands and by many religions. In ancient Egypt, because the lotus grew so plentifully, it became the symbol of reproductive power of all nature and was used in religious rites. From Egypt it was carried to Assyria, and the Greeks dedicated it to the nymphs. Three of India's gods are shown each seated on a great lotus. To Taoists and to China as a whole the lotus is loved and held sacred above all other flowers. To the Buddhists, especially, the lotus is sacred; they introduce it into their sculpture, their painting, and their literature.

Even the cross has not always been uniquely and distinctively Christian. Long before the Christian era it had a prominent place among the many sacred and mystic figures connected with widely scattered mythologies and religions of antiquity. Pre-Christian crosses were thus used in Assyria, Persia, and India, and among some of the Scandinavian peoples of the north, generally with a symbolical religious significance. One of the meanings of the cross was consecration. The Tau form was common in ancient Egypt as a symbol of life. This form is sometimes called, also, the cross of the Old Testament, raised by Moses in the wilderness. Early Christian apologists, when taunted as "cross-worshippers," pointed out that their persecutors themselves adored cruciform objects.

It would seem that the prevalence of the cross, its vitality, and the tenacity with which it has continued through the centuries mark it as a symbol peculiarly adapted to human consciousness. When one considers the central fact in Christianity it would seem inevitable that the cross should become the characteristic symbol of the faith. And yet, there were dangers in adopting the symbol of the cross; historically many of these become actual. For example, many of the early medieval churches had cocks on their steeples. These were often struck by lightning. Gradually the cross was substituted, and the motivating reason in many cases was the supposed efficacy of the cross as protection against all demons and devils. In this and many other such instances the cross was used as a talisman. Moreover, each of the more than fifty forms of the cross used in our churches has its specific name and connotation. Yet because there were such dangers and associations in adopting the cross as a common Christian symbol, is there anyone who would say that the attempt should never have been made to purify and glorify it to become the most central and significant emblem of our faith?

We see, thus, that symbols travel and persist. The swastika, the lotus and the cross are just three examples of how symbols capable of carrying deep meanings are not the private language of any individual, century or religion.

In considering the possible use by Christians of such imagery and artistic stimuli as the insights of mankind have developed one

40

thing is certain—we must be prepared to reject as well as to accept. Unquestionably there will be suggestions that are so contrary to Christian belief and intention as to make any attempt at adaptation unwise. The problem has its acknowledged dangers. Hence lessons from the church history of the West should be combined with the best wisdom of contemporaneous Christian leaders of both East and West in an effort to solve it wisely.

The reason for raising the question of indigenous symbolism is that all are praying for an indigenous church—a church growing naturally, something that will come to feel native and not continue as exotic. The members of the younger churches are to be nationals "in their bones." But it is no light problem to know in what cultural vesture universal truth should be clothed. This matter of symbolism, however, is just a part of that more general problem of fostering a movement that will be faithful to the lessons of Christian history and at the same time will fully express the racial genius and cultural heritage of a given people. No religion that remains borrowed or that is mechanically imitative can ever become powerful enough to change the stream of thought and life in a civilized nation.

Part II : The Worldwide Speech
of Wood and Stone

V : India

Bishop Azariah, of Dornakal, the first Indian Anglican bishop, continues to be a leader in indigenization .(see Nos. 19-20). As the Church of England has given a characteristically English interpretation to catholic Christianity, so he believes the Church of India, Burma and Ceylon should aspire to give a characteristically Indian flavor to that same common faith. He desires that the permanently valuable elements in Indian culture should "be consecrated to the service and worship of the Padma-feet of our Saviour Christ."

Experiments, well established in specific areas, have been made in taking over symbolic ceremonies into Christianity. For example, flowers have been used in worship from time immemorial in India. Some have urged their use in Christian worship as signifying the beauty, creative power and love of God. In several churches flower petals are strewn, Indian fashion, over the congregation as they leave. To the Indian it seems so fitting to offer flowers in worship to God that churches are encouraged to have small gardens, so that fresh flowers may be placed upon the altar. In Kodaikanal, where orchids grow wild by the hundreds, Christians go over the hills just before Easter gathering white orchids to construct into a large cross. In several of the religious paintings by Mr. Alfred D. Thomas, one of the most distinguished Indian Christian painters, a small plant is seen bowing its head to our Lord, signifying that all nature is worshipping. The symbolic use of flowers in Christian worship is by no means general, and just how this can best be done is not yet wholly clear.

Ceremonial bathing before worship is common in India, and facilities for this are generally provided outside mosques and temples. In India, therefore, washing as a symbol of purification is traditional and understood. Hence this symbolism has been adopted by at least a few churches, which have provided pools near their entrances (see Nos. 22, 45).

Moslems and Hindus take off their sandals before entering their mosques and temples as a symbol of reverence. This practice is continued by Christians in many country churches.

In one area candidates for baptism are bidden to turn to the west, the direction of the setting sun—the end of the day being symbolic of the old life of sin, which by their promise they now renounce. Then for the other promises they turn to the east, the direction of the rising sun, the beginning of the new day, symbolizing the beginning of new life.

Christian "Festivals of Lights" are common at the time of *Diwali,* a Hindu festival observed in nearly every part of India. While this festival has certain sinister and idolatrous connections, Hindus think of it as celebrating the triumph of the light of truth over the darkness of ignorance; and for Christians it symbolizes Christ as the Light of the world, or the Bible as the Light-bringer.

In Burma, boys on being admitted to membership in a Buddhist order wear for one day the yellow robe of the monk; so at Kemmendine. a section of Rangoon, white robes of the same pattern are worn for a day after baptism as a sign that they have put on the mantle of the church.

Other symbols are shown in the pictures that follow. For convenience, pictures from Ceylon and from Burma are associated with those from India.

THE CATHEDRAL (*Anglican*), Dornakal, dedicated in 1939, combines several types of architecture.

19. THE EXTERIOR. The twin domes and minarets suggest the Moslem type, since the cathedral is located in an area where the Indo-Saracenic is becoming the rule for public buildings. The supporting pillars are Dravidian (cf. No. 20) because the Christians come from the Dravidian peoples. Finally, the rounded chancel and cross mark the cathedral as Christian. The surrounding wall is typically Indian. Dornakal has long expressed its worship in distinctly Indian forms, and a definite aim in designing the cathedral was to make it harmonize with Indian temple architecture.

20. THE INTERIOR. The Dravidian pillars, with their capitals of Hindu origin, show the drooping, conical banana bud issuing out of the open flower of the datura, or deadly nightshade. The symbolism of this is immediately obvious to anyone familiar with South India, since the banana tree perpetually propagating itself from the same root signifies ever continuing life, and the deadly nightshade is the symbol of death. By inscribing repeatedly on the pillars the cross and the lotus (the symbol to Hindus of the foot of God touching the earth, and to Christians of the incarnation) the symbolism is completed, representing for India a divine Saviour who brought life out of death and ever lives to communicate that life to his followers.

CHRISTU-KULA ASHRAM, Tirupatur. 21. THE EXTERIOR. This Christian
church has been built in the style of Dravidian temple architecture. The general
appearance of the high and ornate *gopurams* (towers) closely resembles those of Hindu
temples. Here the intricate carving, tier upon tier, represents monastic cells indicating
Christian renunciation. The wall incloses a rectangular garden in which is the House
of Prayer amid crotons and coconut palms. There are flower beds; and here and there
are stone seats beside the paths for quiet meditation.

22. CIRCULAR LOTUS POOLS and rectangular tanks for ablutions before worship are seen in front of the House of Prayer on either side.

Dr. S. Jesudason writes: "We do not adopt indigenous expressions as a matter of policy in order to fit in with the national sentiments or currents of the time. Neither do we follow them primarily with some ulterior motive of influencing those around us. We adopt them because it is the natural manner in which we outwardly express our inward devotion to our Lord. Of course, any spontaneous expression of the inner spiritual life is bound to affect others. This is a resultant factor, but our mind is not primarily exercised about that. Deep down within us there is a dynamic spring of inner life tending to burst out and flow through its natural channel."

The Ashram prayer book is called *Jabamalai* ("garland of prayer"). The name of their hymn book, *Paumalai,* means literally "garland of songs"; and one type of service (*archana*) means literally "worshipping with flowers," when songs are sung symbolizing offering the flowers of their hearts to God.

23. THE PILLARS. The *mandapam* type of pillared architecture is followed, with its broad open halls suited to the climate. On the pillars and overhead beams are various carvings of the lotus bearing the cross, the single lotus blossom, vine creepers, flowers and other characteristics of temple carvings. In the capitals note the carvings on either side representing a bunch of plantains hanging from a tree with its flower at the end— here symbolizing deep Christian joy, for it is a South India custom to tie up the plantain with flowers or fruits as a sign of joy at the time of festivals and marriages.

24. THE BEAUTIFULLY CARVED DOORS into the chancel are ordinarily closed, but are open during divine service. The extreme left of the lowest set of panels pictures a garden with a mounted cross that has a vine and grape clusters behind it. The next right shows our Lord talking to Andrew and Philip with John listening. The topic of the discourse is suggested by a sheaf of wheat bending over so that the "corns" of wheat are about to fall into the ground (in the lower right of the panel). The third panel shows our Lord knocking at the door. The extreme lower right symbolizes Christian beauty in life and action. In each of the two central panels of the middle row is a cross coming out of the lotus. The extreme right and left panels of the top row show the vine with grape clusters.

25. THE ALTAR is surmounted by a carved marble slab on which is a large lotus bearing the cross, here standing for the heart of the believer taking in what is meant by the cross of Christ. On the right is a vine with clusters of grapes, and on the left is a stalk of wheat with its "corns" falling into the ground. A dove is in the upper left.

26. THE CHANCEL DOORWAY. Note on the surrounding wall the repetition of the lotus and of the cross surmounting the lotus. On the stone beam over the entrance to the chancel is inscribed in Tamil this sentence: "God forbid that I should glory save in the cross of Jesus Christ my Lord." The upright brass lamps on either side of the altar burn while all the other lights are out, betokening the light of God, which illumines this dark world, shining more and more unto the perfect day. Two small slit-like openings in the folding doors enable visitors to look within this dimly lighted chancel when the doors are shut.

27. SOUTH INDIAN CHRISTIAN HOUSEHOLD LAMPS. Most Hindu lamps of this type bear either a figure of Lakshmi flanked by a pair of elephants, or a tripartite symbol flanked by the sun and moon. The central one above shows a Christian form of this kind of household lamp, in which the cross is flanked by a pair of attendant angels. Usually the Christian type bears only the cross, as in the other two pictures. These three specimens are in the Government Museum, Madras.

THE CHAPEL, TRINITY COLLEGE (*C.M.S.*), Kandy, Ceylon. The floor of this beautiful chapel, embodying many elements of Singhalese architecture, is flanked on either side by a double row of gigantic pillars. There are fifty of these columns, making a forest of sixteen-foot monoliths—square based, square capped, but the main stem octagonal.

28. THE LOTUS is carved on many of the square faces of the capitals.

29. THE KANDYAN LION is the mythical ancestor and totem animal of the Singhalese, standing for majesty and power. This particular lion is found on the crest of Trinity College.

30. THE SACRED SWAN is the Singhalese emblem of wisdom.

31. A PEKADA. Above each pillar is a kind of super-capital much used in India and Ceylon. The design roughly resembles four bells, the mouth of each bell carved with a full-blown inverted lotus.

32. THE LIYA POTA. The exceedingly conventional foliar ornament is more characteristic of Singhalese design than any other form. Instruction in the use of it is almost the first thing taught to young craftsmen.

33. CLERGY STALL. The carvings over the arch represent a *liya thorana,* a local vine-leaf design in which are found two birds (hopees). The border is another local vine (*liya vela*)—traditional Kandyan patterns.

This chapel is Trinity's alabaster box of ointment, poured forth to associate not only beauty with worship, but also religion with race and culture. In detail and as a whole this chapel is a beautiful and meaningful symbol.

28. THE LOTUS   29. THE KANDYAN LION

30. THE SACRED SWAN

31. A PEKADA

32. THE LIYA POTA

33. CLERGY STALL

THE CHAPEL OF THE TRANSFIGURATION, BISHOP'S THEO-
LOGICAL COLLEGE (*Anglican*), Tirumaraiyur. This chapel, begun in 1938,
embodies many elements of local Hindu architecture as to both general plan and
detailed carving. A lofy *gopuram* (tower) stands above the altar, the pulpit is a small,
Indian-type dais, and the nave is in the form of an open-air courtyard with roofed-in
aisles. The architect, the Reverend G. E. Hubbard, has taken forms hitherto consecrated to "the God whom ye ignorantly worship" and has offered them to God as
revealed in Jesus Christ. He hopes that, by thus blending designs common to certain
great Hindu temples in the district with what is unmistakably Christian, there may
be a far-reaching effect on the future clergy of South India.

The sixteen pillars of the courtyard have three designs on each of their four faces,
while each capital has two different designs. This means that in the courtyard, alone,
there are no fewer than 224 carved emblems. While South India temple forms have
been freely used, yet, because of the way in which Hindu mythology permeates temple
symbolism, the greatest care has been taken not to introduce any actual symbolism from
Hinduism with the exception of two items:

34. THE WHEEL is found on many of the capitals of the
chapel. This design is frequently seen on the local country-
cart axle-stocks, and is sometimes mistaken for the lotus.
The wheel symbolizes that life is a journey through time
with the hope of rest at the journey's end.

35-36. THE BANANA-BUD CAPITALS illustrate life out of death, the bud emerging
from the poison flower.

37-38. THE PILLARS. While, apart from the wheel and banana-bud, no Hindu symbolism finds a place in this chapel, the type of pillars on which the distinctively Christian symbolism appears is definitely Hindu. This is at once evident by comparing three
pillars of this chapel (No. 38) with a section of the interior of the Alwartirunagari
temple, which was the chapel's prototype (No. 37). Obviously the general style is
the same, Hindu detail being displaced by non-Hindu symbols. These consist of classical
Christian designs with allegorical, doctrinal, metaphysical or historical meanings, as
well as of local plants and beasts, and the arms of the various colleges and universities
represented by the local missionaries. For example, the nearest pillar in No. 38 was
presented by the Art Industrial School, of Nazareth, and hence at the bottom one
sees the saw and square of carpentry; a blacksmithing section at the center; and an
automobile at the top to represent the motoring section. The right-hand pillar in No.
38, being the gift of St. John's College, Palamcottah, shows emblems of various
apostles as found in medieval art—the diagonal cross of St. Andrew in the shadow
at the top; the V-shaped frame of wood, symbol of his traditional death, at the center;
and, at the bottom, two crossed fishes, recalling Andrew's original occupation and his
call to become a fisher of men.

Eight of the pillars were gifts of groups in the Tinnevelly Diocese. The masons'
pillar was given in varying sums from their weekly wages by the Hindu workmen
engaged on the chapel. Christian villages turned out *en masse* to haul, along with
bullocks, on the ropes which dragged the heavy monoliths over rough country roads.
Enthusiasm prevailed such as must have characterized England of the Middle Ages
when a village church was being built.

35. UPPER ARCHWAY

36. BANANA-BUD CAPITAL

37. SECTION OF HINDU TEMPLE

38. CORRESPONDING SECTION OF THE CHAPEL

39. A SYMBOL OF MOTHERHOOD. The cow and calf is often used by Alfred D. Thomas, an outstanding Indian Christian painter, to represent motherhood, as here, in his picture of "The Nativity."

40. THE LOTUS OFFERING. In "The Adoration of the Shepherds," by Alfred
D. Thomas, the Virgin Mary is represented as sitting under a tree by the edge of a
stream and holding the Holy Child in her lap. She has the features of a high-caste
Hindu lady. Before her kneels a shepherd who has the dress of a peasant of Northern
India, and who bears in his hands a white lotus. One of the farther figures is carrying
an earthernware pot with lotus buds in it. The lotus is the traditional offering of a
Hindu to his god, implying a rendering up of one's own existence to its Source—a
resignation of one's own nature and ground for separate existence.

41. PULPIT TABLE, MEMORIAL HOSPITAL FOR WOMEN AND CHILDREN (*United Presbyterian*), Sialkot. A local artisan has carved a pomegranate pattern in *sheesham* wood for the pulpit table in the chapel of this hospital. Not only does the pomegranate, because of its numerous seeds, stand in Western symbolism for fruitfulness, plenty and God's blessing; but in Hindu temples pomegranates are used as offerings to the gods in an appeal for blessing. Indians also associate this fruit with healing because of its medicinal value—another reason for its choice for a hospital design.

42. WINDOWS, CHURCH AT BHAVNAGAR (*Irish Presbyterian*), Kathiawar. In these two windows of pierced stone, so characteristic of India, are set forth the symbols of Christian worship. Above in the left window is the shamrock, and in the right, the lotus, emblematic of Ireland and of India united in the worship of Christ. Below one may see the harp of praise; the censer of prayer; the Word shown as scroll, sword, hammer (*Jeremiah* 23: 29), lamp and shield; and the sacrament of the Lord's Supper indicated by the wheat sheaf and vine.

43. UNION THEOLOGICAL SEMINARY, Tumkur. The main door of the seminary chapel is of a kind generally found in temples and *matts,* and the decorative motif on this door as well as on the reading desk is the cross superimposed on the lotus. At Tumkur this design is meant to suggest that in the circle of the white lotus (circle for infinity, and lotus for purity) is fulfilled the infinite and holy love of God through the historic fact of the Cross of Jesus Christ.

The cruciform window to the right is at the back of the chancel, and by means of the open, pierced work shows the vine, grapes and branches. As the congregation looks through this glassless window the waving green branches of the near-by tree make the cross with its vine no dead thing, but full of movement, light and life.

HOUSE OF PRAYER (*Ref. Ch. in America*), Vellore. 44. THE PILLARS. The left-hand pillar carries Hindu symbols. At the bottom is the peacock, which seems to be the only creature which takes delight in Nature's terrible thunder before a storm. It therefore symbolizes joy in God's mighty power even in the darkest hour of deepest need. Above the peacock is a swan, here used as a symbol of perfect discernment—the ability to distinguish the essential from the non-essential—since the swan is supposed to be able to separate milk from water when the two are mixed. Early Hindu writers emphasize that in religion the pure should be separated from the dross even as the swan draws out the milk from the water. At the top is the lotus.

The central column carries Christian symbols—at the bottom, the grapevine; next above, entwined vines indicating that our lives should be linked with God's; at the top, trefoils for the Trinity.

At the bottom of the right-hand pillar is the cross surmounting the lotus, which indicates for this House of Prayer that Christianity is the fulfillment of Hinduism. This symbol is carved on each pillar of the chapel. At the top is a mango blossom, an Indian symbol of the promise of fruit, and hence here of abundance from the hand of God and of new bursting into life.

45. THE LOTUS TANK. The water from this lotus tank is used for cleansing the feet of worshippers before entering the House of Prayer.

46. THE CHANCEL. On the steps is a deer skin upon which (after the Indian custom) the religious teacher sits while preaching. Beside the deer skin is an adaptation of a Moslem Koran stand upon which the Bible rests. On either side of the central cross is a tall Indian lamp surmounted by a brazen "torch of fire," here symbolic of the coming of the Holy Spirit with new life.

47. THE BAPTISMAL BOWL. This lotus bowl was originally made for a Hindu temple; but is here used as a baptismal bowl. In medieval Christian times, also, holy water fonts were not infrequently made from antique objects—urns or hollowed pillars— thus serving a purpose other than that for which they were originally intended.

48. CHRIST, THE BURDEN BEARER. In the tower over the chancel in the Christu-kula (Family-of-Christ) Ashram at Tirupatur (see Nos. 21-27) is a symbol of the Christ growing out of the local environment. In the center one sees a large, shady tree with its branches, leaves and blossoms. A pigeon rests in the shade on the trunk. At the foot of the tree sits a tired man; but his happy face shows that he has inward peace. For, immediately to the left is a representation of the burden bearer, so common on the dusty roads of South India—two upright slabs of stone with another stone across the top. On this the weary man has placed his heavy burden. It is meant to recall the Christ who said, "Come unto me, all ye that labor and are heavy laden, and I will give you rest." With this should be compared another interpretation of this symbol in No. 7.

49. **SEAL OF THE INCORPORATED TRUSTEES OF THE CHURCH OF INDIA, BURMA AND CEYLON.** St. Thomas, the Apostle of India, is in the center. On the left, an elephant for India; on the right, the peacock in glory, for Burma; beneath, a group of palms, for Ceylon. The coats of arms that follow on this and the next page are all Anglican, also.

50. **DIOCESE OF DORNAKAL.** The lotus enters this design as the Indian national flower. Hence the distinctive Christian symbol at the center of the lotus is saying that the cross is situated at the heart of India.

51. **DIOCESE OF CHOTA NAGPUR.** This shows four flaming Indian *chirags* (lamps), along with other obvious Christian symbolism.

CRESTS AND SEALS IN INDIA (*continued*)

52. DIOCESE OF RANGOON.

53. DIOCESE OF LAHORE. The sun rises behind the snowy Himalayas. Below are the five rivers of the Punjab (literally, "five waters").

54. DIOCESE OF NAGPUR. The name of the diocese suggests the choice of symbol, since Nagpur means "cobra city." The cross, emblematic of the faith, rises over the serpent, emblematic of the powers of evil.

55. DIOCESE OF MADRAS. The banyan tree, dropping roots into the soil from its widely spreading branches, is symbolic of the missionary work of the church. The lion and the lamb lying down together and the dove represent Christian peace.

56. DIOCESE OF TINNEVELLY. This shows the cross and the paddy (rice) plant, the staple food of the people. The wavy lines at the bottom are intended to represent the field in which the rice plants are growing. Tinnevelly means "holy-paddy-hedge," and the name comes from a town wholly surrounded by rice fields.

57. DIOCESE OF LUCKNOW. The castle represents the Residency at Lucknow, famed for its defense in the Mutiny of 1857. The flag remains flying all day and night and is never taken down except to be changed. The three bands across the shield represent the two great rivers of the province, the Ganges and the Jumna, which join at Allahabad with a legendary third underground river.

58. DIOCESE OF NASIK. In this famine-stricken area wells are the chief supply of water; hence four are represented on the coat of arms. Furthermore, a cross springs out of each well in accord with the Latin motto, *Natis aqua salus in cruce* (There is salvation in the cross for those who are born of water). With this is associated, also, *Isaiah* 12:2: "Therefore with joy shall ye draw water out of the wells of salvation." The initial letters of the Latin motto form the diocesan name "Nasik." The large diagonal cross on the shield is that of St. Andrew, since he is the patron saint of the diocese.

59. DIOCESE OF ASSAM. The wavy lines are symbolical of the rivers and plains of Assam, over which the church's work is to spread the message of the cross; hence a red cross is superimposed on lines of blue and silver. The staple industry of the diocese is the production of tea, and therefore branches of the tea bush are shown on either side of the miter.

66

52   53   54

55   56

57   58   59

CRESTS AND SEALS IN INDIA (*continued*)

60. FORMAN CHRISTIAN COLLEGE (*Union*), Lahore. The Punjab (literally "five waters") takes its name from the five great rivers of that province of India. Thus the sun is seen rising over the province under the influence of the open Bible, on which is seen the first and last letter of the Greek alphabet, the apocalyptic Alpha and Omega, signifying that the Lord Jesus is the beginning and the end of all things.

61. THE CENTENNIAL SCHOOL (*Methodist*), Lucknow. The circular band consists of leaves beneath scrolls; these leaves signify the ever abundant generosity of nature in India's climate. For this school the lotus flower at the left stands for India's art; the swastika at the right,. for her philosophies. The sun at the center, superimposed on the map of India, recalls a motto on India's coinage, "Heaven's Light our Guide," but may also be thought of as the "Sun of Righteousness." The cross superimposed on the map is the symbol of love, service and sacrifice.

62. THE KAREN THEOLOGICAL SEMINARY (*Baptist*), Insein, Burma. The open volume pictured in this seal represents the Lost Book of the Karen people of Burma. There had been a widespread tradition, still current among the people when Adoniram Judson and his colleagues went to Burma, to the effect that one day their long-absent "white brother" would return to them from across the great waters, bringing their Lost Book, which they had long looked for with unabated expectation. They accepted the religious books of the white missionaries. "At the sight of this unspeakable treasure some of those present bowed down and worshipped, others wept, some touched and caressed the sacred book, some kissed it, and some gazed long and curiously at its title. They crowded around the volume so thickly that the chief lifted it high above his head, in order that all might see, and all gazed at it with bated breath. With the return of their book through the white brother they were no longer to be a despised nation."

63. LEONARD THEOLOGICAL COLLEGE (*Methodist*), Jubbulpore. An attempt has been made to express the spirit and purpose of this seminary in its shield. As a whole it suggests the gospel of Jesus Christ at the heart of India. The lotus represents the beautiful spiritual heritage of India and aspiration for the Divine—the heart of India. The Moslem type of arch suggests Islam and the ancient glories of Indian history. At the center is the cross, which is the heart of the Christian message. The cross meets the need of the heart of India (hence the cross implanted in the lotus), and should represent the spirit of India's ministers. Only in the strength of Christ can this ideal be realized; hence the two Greek words meaning, "Living Way" (*Hebrews* 10:20). This thought is suggested, also, by the grapevine on each side above the arch. The vine signifies, also, fellowship with Christ (*John* 15:1-4). From the Christian standpoint the archway represents the open door of opportunity in India today, with the cross the secret of that opportunity. It involves the building of the church of ideal beauty, suggested by the arch's proportions, which were taken from the most beautiful building in India, the Taj Mahal. The initials of the name of the college are worked into the vine—thus binding the institution together in Christ.

68

60

61

62

63

64. THE KELLY HIGH SCHOOL (*Baptist*), Mandalay. The outer circle symbolizes life unbroken. Within this is the shield of the Christian faith, and in the center the cross of sacrifice. On one side is the lamp of enlightenment; and on the other an open book, for intellectual attainments. Since enlightenment and intellectual attainment receive much emphasis in Buddhism, as values that come from within the man and yet not entirely without his exertion, the design is thought to combine the best in Christianity with an outstanding ideal of Buddhism.

65. KOINONIA. The badge of the Burma Gospel Team, and the design on its temporary magazine, *Koinonia* (Fellowship), has as its center the peacock, the national emblem of Burma, here symbolizing God-controlled Christian nationalism. The "3" at the top stands for the three principles of "expert friendship"—friendship with God, with each other, and with *all* others. On either side are the initial letters of "Gospel Team." To the right is the Star of Bethlehem, our only hope, while the number to the left recalls "Paul's sixty-seven friends in Christ." The Burmese word at the bottom means "eternal life."

66. JUDSON COLLEGE (*Baptist*), Rangoon. The basic symbols in this design used as the official seal of the college and as a badge on sport jackets, etc., are the cross and Bible, to indicate that the college is Christian, and the peacock (the national emblem of Burma), to indicate its location in Burma. The twelve lotus buds were not intended to refer to any specific religion, but were added as representing the spiritual aspiration of the East (the number twelve is without other than artistic significance). Some effort has been made to associate with the peacock its early Christian significance (originally adapted from pagan mythology), when it was a popular symbol of the resurrection and also of immortality. The peacock is said to shed his brilliant feathers annually, after which he has new feathers, finer and more brilliant than before.

67. EVANGELICAL-LUTHERAN THEOLOGICAL COLLEGE, Madras. On the wall of the chapel of this *gurukul,* or seminary, is a painting from which its seal was copied. The lotus pond represents India. In Hinduism the lotus flower, itself, represents the seat of Sarasvathi, the Goddess of Knowledge; here, in connection with the cross, it represents the seat of Divine Wisdom. From an invisible rock under the surface of blue water rises a golden cross signifying that the precious and unique gospel of Christ is deeply rooted in India. At the center of the cross is the Luther rose (since Luther rediscovered the true meaning of the cross), from which golden rays flash in all directions. This snow-white rose with five petals on a golden ground has a red heart in the center of which is a small black cross signifying (according to an old German rhyme) that the heart of a Christian is walking on roses only when it is living under the cross.

The chapel picture and the seal, therefore, speak this message: The cross of Christ is planted right in the midst of the vast Indian nation (represented by the limitless lotus sea). On the unseen rock, which is Christ, the Christian church of the Lutheran type is founded.

70

64

65

66

67

68. ST. LUKE S SCHOOL (*Baptist*), Toungoo, Burma. The initials of the school appear at the center, out from which goes the cross (red in the original), completed in the swastika, which is recognized by the school as an Aryan emblem of the father of the gods, as well as having been used by the Greeks, the Latins, the Buddhists in China and the Christians in France, Germany and England. The circles are used as a symbol of eternity and the Divine, of fellowship and unity. The Latin motto, "Many in One," teaches the students that unity means harmony of differences as opposed to uniformity implying sameness.

69. ST. COLUMBA'S COLLEGE (*Anglican*), Hazaribagh, Chota Nagpur. On the lower left is seen the rising sun of righteousness and the sower sowing the seed, indicating the work of the Society for the Propagation of the Gospel. On the bottom right the location of the college is symbolically represented. Hazaribagh, Chota Nagpur means in Hindu "a thousand tigers, small-snake city"; hence M, tiger, snake. On the top left is a *columba* (Latin for dove), holding a shamrock, symbol of the Trinity. On the top right are the arms of Dublin University, since this college is under the Dublin University Mission.

70. ST. JOSEPH'S COLLEGE (*Roman Catholic*), Trichinopoly. There is history, stimulation from saint veneration, local reference and Christian purpose in this shield. Trichinopoly is famous for a great rock near by, shown on the lower left with a Hindu temple on top. On the lower right is a Christian church surmounted by the cross. Between is the college witnessing from one to the other. The cross on the church faces the temple in a contest that is spiritual—hence the overarching bow. The college was founded by the Society of Jesuits, represented by the monogram at the top of the shield—JHS (an abbreviation of the Greek name of "Jesus"), with the cross above and three rough nails with square heads below signifying the passion. Since the college was named after St. Joseph (spouse of the Virgin Mary), this saint's emblems appear above the shield—the lily, since according to ancient legend his staff blossomed with lilies; the crown, since in ecclesiastical usage the saints are portrayed thus to symbolize their reigning with Christ.

71. SCHOOL AT SRINAGAR (*C. M. S.*). Srinagar might be called the Venice of Kashmir, for the main street of the city and many of the side ones are made by the river Jhelum, upon which long, slender boats are propelled by means of characteristic, heart-shaped paddles. Since this boys' school is alongside the river traffic, paddles were chosen to stand for self-reliance and sturdy, hard work; and their broad, heart-shaped blades for large-hearted sympathy and fellow-feeling. The paddles are crossed to remind men of Him who made self-sacrifice even unto death the bedrock of his life and purpose, and service to mankind the one dominating motive of his earthly existence. The school motto, as well as the crest, embodies the school's ideal of manhood.

72

68

69

DOMINE DU S HABITABIT?

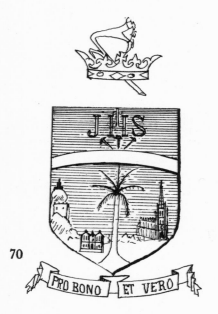

70

PRO BONO ET VERO

71

72. THE WOMEN'S CHRISTIAN COLLEGE, Madras, has a pin very popular with the girls because of its beauty in color and symbolism. The college motto is "Lighted to Lighten" and hence the appropriateness of the little earthenware Indian lamp still used in temple decoration and in the evening worship of a home. From such a lamp, with its flake of fire constantly renewed by the sacrifice of the oil poured in, its need of shelter from the wind, its flame kindled afresh every evening from a source of light, comes the suggestion of a life spending itself to transform its wealth into service, flickering but not failing in the midst of temptation, existing only to give.

The college flower is the sunflower, chosen because it always turns its face toward the sun, suggesting that we should ever turn to the Sun of Righteousness. The sunflower is chosen, also, because it is a compositæ, thus symbolizing a group such as a college community; and because it grows readily in all three lands associated with the college—India, England and America. Still further, the sunflower embodies the college colors—green representing India's palms and paddy fields; brown, her sunburnt soil; and gold, the flame of the college lamp.

In the chapel of this college, hanging from a curve in the apse, is a large lamp of Indian design, a sphere of perforated brass—a second symbol of the college motto, "Lighted to Lighten." From dusk to bedtime it sends forth its glow. Being an electric light it needs no oil, it hangs secure in the very path of the monsoon rain and wind, at a touch its golden radiance springs out of darkness—a symbol of ready help. Attention is called to the fact that its brightness depends on the slender thread hardly noticed at first, which connects the fragile filament hidden inside the lamp with the power house miles away where vast funds of energy are stored for the lighting of Madras. The lamp speaks of a life of service maintained by prayer, by contact with hidden sources of light, a life of strength all-powerful if the union is kept, but dark and useless if the contact with the grace of God is broken.

Many of the girls go forth to villages where the churches may be very plain and simple compared with their college chapel. "True," as one chapel sermon observed, "but from this place you should carry such a passion for beauty that you will do your utmost to make your village church a more lovely place."

74

VI : China

One of the most distinctive and characteristic features of Chinese art is the symbolic character of its expression. China has a wealth of such material to which the people are sensitive. There is scarcely a design so slight as to have no meaning. "A spray of flowering plum or hibiscus trembling in the wind could be as significant to the spirit as the forms of deity or angel." However, relatively few distinctively Chinese symbols have been widely used by Christians.

Various reasons are given for this situation. For one thing, it is hard to persuade congregations in bare halls that anything more is needed or desirable. To some, Chinese motifs would suggest idolatry and paganism. An inquirer might get the impression that the new religion is simply the old one under another guise. A more serious reason may be that the greater part of Chinese symbolism has been concerned with happiness brought about by material prosperity. As will be seen in the explanations given later in connection with the illustrations, distinctive Chinese symbols gather around such human desires as long life, wealth, children, happiness. There is also the prevailing belief that emblems of happy import themselves help to confer the blessings they represent. On the other hand, Luke Ch'en, the Christian president of the Academy of Fine Arts at the Catholic University of Peiping, says that the church must "show itself as sympathetic, not as anti-Chinese . . . and that all artistic expression must be avoided which would give the church the stamp of something foreign and which would be unacceptable to those who have formed their taste and their mentality in the Orient."

However, it is interesting to see just what Christian symbolism is used in China. The carp on the church roof-ridge is used with the Chinese significance of courage, of perseverance, of struggle against the current. Large wall crosses behind the chancel are often painted red to signify joy in redemption. The Anglican Cathedral in Peiping has for a font a deep fishbowl of cream-colored glazed stoneware. Sometimes such bowls display a butterfly design, another symbol of joy (since the butterfly flits hither and thither supping nectar from countless flowers). The three Magi are shown as three symbolic figures betokening Confucianism, Buddhism and Taoism bringing their gifts to the infant Jesus (cf. *Each with His Own Brush,* p. 18). In Peiping, a worship service is built about the use of yellow, red and white candles. Yellow was the imperial color; and lighting this candle is a symbol of making God the king of life during the year ahead. The red candle symbolizes that we should take God into all our joys, since red in China stands for joy and happiness. White in China stands for sorrow and mourning, and so lighting the white candle betokens our desire to take our difficulties and sorrows to God. Other examples are pictured and explained in the pages that follow.

If we are to understand and to delight in any traditional art, whether it be of China, the Middle Ages, or that of other folk in any time or part of the world, we must learn the relevant language of expression—not merely record our reactions to it. For instance, note the three examples of Salvator Mundi Dominus (Lord Saviour of the World) below. In the center of each of the two designs to the right are three crosses. In Chinese the number 10 is shaped like a cross, so that the three crosses can stand for thirty, and hence for a generation. Thus man should realize that through his whole life he ought to bear the cross and in this way make perfect in his body the redemption of Christ. The dove in the design to the left indicates that the Holy Spirit cooperates with the Redeemer for our salvation. The ideographic symbols on the left in each design are quite similar and stand for "Lord." The symbols on the right in each case represent "Saviour," this being accomplished in the middle design by a conventionalized wheat stock and grape cluster. The suggestion for "world" is easily recognized. The three-leaf designs indicate the Trinity; and the four-leaf design, the cross.

CHINESE LATTICE. Chinese lattice windows have a beauty that has satisfied a people for three thousand years. The striking variations, so diverse and so perfectly proportioned, with historic as well as artistic meaning, form an authentic branch of Chinese art. Dr. Daniel Sheets Dye, of West China Union University, has reproduced nearly twenty-five hundred of these designs in his *Grammar of Chinese Lattice*. Some of the patterns have symbolic connotations, but in all there is a gripping appeal of line and design characteristic of China's cultural sphere. So far as the writer has been able to discover, very few churches have drawn upon this rich and fascinating heritage.

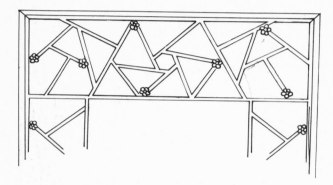

73. THE BREAK-UP OF ICE is suggested by this pattern (Presbyterian Church, Show-chow). To appreciate such ice designs one should observe ice forming on quiet water on a cold night, or the lines formed by cracking ice. The plum blossom, also, symbolizes spring.

74. THIS "MAN-CHARACTER ICE RAY" was designed for the window of the bursar's office of West China Union University. The old Chinese character for "man" is something like the letter "T" and is found repeatedly in this design (cf. No. 78).

75. CIRCLE OF HEAVEN

76. SQUARE OF EARTH

77. SIX CONCENTRIC GREEK CROSSES

78. MAN CHARACTER (T)

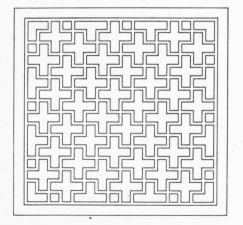

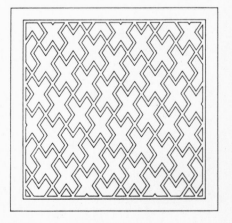

79-80. THE SWASTIKA formed by the bar outlines has popularity in certain areas quite apart from Buddhism. The open voids give the Greek and the Saltire cross, respectively.

GOLDBEATERS' STREET CHURCH (First Baptist Church of Chengtu). An old Chinese building of about A.D. 1700 was rebuilt for this church by Dr. Dye, assisted by the pastor, the Reverend Fu Chin-beh. Every effort was made to keep the building simple, yet richly Chinese. The five windows to the left in No. 83 incorporate the circle of heaven (cf. No. 75) and the square of earth (cf. No. 76). The window to the right in this picture, immediately back of the pulpit, again uses the symbols for heaven and earth, but adds a border that repeatedly incorporates the T symbol for man (cf. No. 78). This window, therefore, stands for three realities—heaven, earth, man. The Chinese inscriptions about the window are in black lacquer on gold foil boards embodying texts about God (above), Christ (below), and on the sides "Thou shalt love the Lord thy God with all thy heart, etc."; or, God, Christ, man. All these windows were designed by Dr. Dye.

81. AN "ICE-CRACK" WINDOW is shown with the circle of heaven.

82. THE MING MOON DOOR of the side guest hall pictures the circle, again bespeaking heaven; and the rectangular squares in the grille on either side embody the "sovereign earth" symbol. The old crape myrtle tree, possibly over two hundred years old, is "splendidly beautiful with its pink blossoms."

81. "ICE-CRACK" WINDOW

82. MING MOON DOOR

83. INTERIOR

PRESBYTERIAN CHURCH, Showchow. High up on either side of the chancel of this church are the two beautifully carved panels shown on this and the following page. The flowers of the four seasons seen in the panels are full of rich symbolism for the Chinese.

84. On the left of this picture are bamboos (winter); on the right, chrysanthemums (fall).

85. On the right are plum blossoms (spring); on the left, summer flowers. This church (a memorial to Mrs. Emily Schell), beautiful in Chinese design and coloring, has great pillars in rich Chinese red and many other carvings depicting scenes in the life of Christ. Over the communion table, against a background of jade-colored tile, is a golden cross.

TAO FONG SHAN CHRISTIAN INSTITUTE, Shatin. On a high point near Hongkong, the Reverend Karl Ludwig Reichelt, a Scandinavian Lutheran, has established a Christian monastery in an effort to lead Buddhists to faith in Jesus Christ as the only one in whom the profound ideals of Buddhism find their complete fulfillment. The Chinese name means "truth, wind, hill'—i.e., Hill of the Spirit of Truth.

86. THE INTERIOR OF THE CHURCH.

87. THE ALTAR bears in the center of the top panel the Sun of Righteousness, on either side of which are wings with their healing power. At the center of the middle panel is a triangle, symbol of the Trinity, inclosing the swastika, betokening cosmic harmony. To the left is the XP symbol for Christ, and to the right an incense burner with the holy fire. On the lowest panel at the center is the monastery's special symbol—the cross on a lotus; the willow and jar of living water, on the right; and on the left, the fruit-bearing lotus. The four feet of the altar are fishes, recalling the Greek acrostic signifying "Jesus Christ, Son of God, Saviour," an emblem of profound significance to early Christians. The smoke from the incense burner between the red candles rises up as a symbol of aspiration.

88. THE BAPTISMAL FONT represents an opened lotus, whose cover is a seven-storied pagoda, indicating development from plane to plane under the sacred cross.

89. THE SPECIAL SYMBOL OF THE MONASTERY signifies the truth that, through Jesus Christ and his cross, men may open the lotus of their hearts, becoming born again and coming in touch with the Divine and Eternal. Curiosity concerning this symbol gives Dr. Reichelt many opportunities to present the message of the regeneration of the human heart by faith in God through Jesus.

90. ABOVE THE ENTRANCE TO THE CHANCEL of the Prayer Hall one sees on the wall the sun with its seven cardinal beams (the seven Spirits of God). Below, lotus flowers become more and more open as they are nearer the sun.

87. THE TEMPLE ALTAR

88. THE BAPTISMAL FONT

89. THE MONASTERY SYMBOL

90. ABOVE THE ENTRANCE TO THE CHANCEL

THE MI SHIH CHURCH OF CHRIST IN CHINA, Peiping. The most interesting thing about this church is the story of its refurnishing. For years its pastor, the Reverend Mr. Chang, had suffered from the bare unattractiveness of an ugly church interior, and especially from the large, unadorned, box-like, empty chancel. This situation grated also on Miss Hazel F. Bailey, an American Congregational missionary, who kept visioning how this storeroom-like chancel might be changed into a place of dignity and beauty. There was no money, and therefore many sheafs of simple plans were made for painting, or appliquéing, false windows or Gothic arches on the great expanse of back wall—only to be laid aside as unsatisfactory. Just when a quiet place was most needed for the congregation to gain strength in the face of fire, murder, plunder and famine an unexpected cheque came from a woman's missionary society in Dekalb, Illinois.

With the aid of the twenty-year-old son of the pastor a search began in all the nooks of the jumbled, little, dirt-floor shops full of second-hand bits of carving, partitions and railings. These odds and ends began to look like gold veins in a mine. In this way the chancel furnishings were found and pieced together, scarcely two parts from the same shop.

91. THE CHANCEL. Above the central altar cross is an arched frame for the altar curtain, beautifully carved with loosely scrolled leaves (symbol of happiness), and at the joints between the arches carved with grape clusters (symbol of every good thing—children, wealth, age). For this church this design is a reminder of the "vine and branches." A Chinese symbol at the center of this frame was replaced by a cross in gold, which even in this picture shines out like a star above the curtain.

On either side of the altar curtain and extending to the side walls is a series of panels once used as a partition in a large Chinese house. On these panels can be detected a swastika pattern. Here it is interpreted as a cross form and hence an appropriate background for the chancel.

Carved panels embodying the scrolled leaf and grape design were found from which the pulpit on the left and the organ screen on the right were made. To the original altar table, in Ming dynasty style, three panels were added with a cross design on each.

92. REAR VIEW OF THE PULPIT. The Chinese words, incised in gold, which face the minister before he rises to speak mean, "Sir, I would see Jesus." How could anyone who has a consecrated imagination face those words through the worship service and then rise to preach anything but Jesus and his way of life? Similarly, on the low carved screens that are in front of each section of the choir (not shown) are the Chinese words for "Set apart, holy unto the Lord," also incised in gold.

When the congregation saw the beauty of the transformed chancel they contributed funds over and above the original gift for labor; and later for the redecorating of the entire interior to harmonize with the new chancel.

84

91. ABOVE THE CHANCEL

92. REAR VIEW OF THE PULPIT

ST. MARY'S CHURCH (*Anglican*), Causeway Bay, Hongkong. A new Chinese church, St. Mary's, has been built in Hongkong under the leadership of the Bishop of Hongkong, the Right Reverend R. O. Hall. The symbolism was designed by an able helper, Mr. Yuan Hsi Kuo.

93. THE CHURCH.

94. A HAND-CARVED CHOIR CHAIR shows the cross at the top, with lotus flowers immediately below at either side. Between the lotus flowers is the symbol for "success to heart's desire." In the center below are mountains, with symbols for waves of water on either side, standing for Hongkong. At the extreme right are chrysanthemums.

95. ON THE ALTAR the five central panels embody, from right to left, the following symbols: wheat, bread, the cross, the Bible, and a flower. Below at the extreme right and left as well as in the center are lotus flowers. To the left of the central lotus is a bird and jar of holy water; to the right, a lotus leaf and a fish.

94. A CHOIR CHAIR

95. THE ALTAR

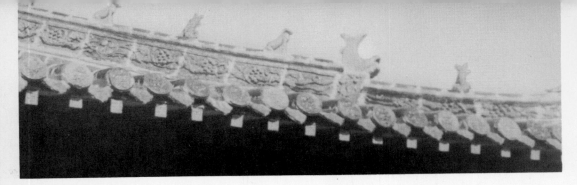

THE PRESBYTERIAN CHURCH, Nanhsuchow. This church, both within and without, is a beautiful example of Chinese architecture. On the end of each large truss beam the cross is worked in green and yellow tiles. The work under the eaves is entirely Chinese and is painted in dark red. The doors are Chinese in design and are likewise painted dark red. Inside, the most striking feature is the set of sixteen vermilion pillars twenty-eight feet high. On the various beams are fifteen large carved wooden panels painted in delicate shades, depicting various scenes in the life of our Lord. The idea back of this church was to interpret Christian truth through Chinese art and construction, while the whole church symbolizes "bringing the best to God." Notice the color in the detail which follows.

96. ON THE RIDGE are Chinese "lions" and at other places conventionalized figures of the dove, lamb and fish. Just below these animals is the grapevine. Below this on each of the circular ends of the rafters is the "Ai" character for "love," which takes the place of the cat in local temples. On each of the square ends of the lowest wooden beams, painted in white, is the swastika in echelon, meaning for some of the local people "long life."

97. THE PANELS OF THE CEILING show on a background of maroon large white cranes in full flight—birds that are so steady and high in their flight that it is said they reach heaven. Around the light socket are cloud designs for decorations. Green, red and gold enter into this color scheme.

98-99. ABOVE THE CHANCEL are two carved and perforated panels. At the bottom of each are the cross and the grapevine. In the upper right-hand corner of No. 99 is the pine tree which is always green—never changing. In the middle of No. 98 is *lan tsao,* a very fragrant grass which gives off its perfume to anything with which it comes in contact, just as a good man's influence can be felt even after one leaves him. At the right of No. 98 are plum blossoms, flowering in early spring, unafraid of hardships. At the upper left in No. 99 is the bamboo, like a good man growing very straight and with no evil at his heart. To the right in No. 99 is the chrysanthemum, which shows its beauty in the late fall after other flowers have gone.

100. THE CHRISTIAN FISH appears at the end of each ridge, supported on the lotus flower.

101. CARVED BRICK PANELS may be seen on the sides of the entrance to the church. One panel was damaged by bombing and this one was cracked. It is a typical Chinese picture, lightly traced in black and gold, of a mountain with a road leading up to it. Its significance is at once suggested by the Chinese words meaning "way, truth, life."

96

97

98

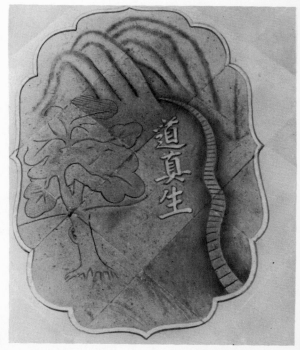

99

TWINEM MEMORIAL PRAYER HALL, UNIVERSITY OF NANKING.

This beautiful chapel is devoted exclusively to prayer, meditation and individual interviews, and is never closed day or night. The donors desired a house of God expressed in the architectural language of the people who use it. The pictures on this and the following pages give some idea of the satisfying extent to which this ideal has been attained.

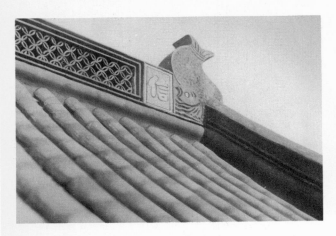

102. RIDGE WITH FISH AND "FAITH" CHARACTER

103. CROSS AND CHARACTER FOR "LOVE"

104. LECTERN WITH CROSS ON LOTUS

105. KNEELING STAND WITH CROSS ON LOTUS

106. TEMPLE BELL AND WINDOWS;
FISH ON RIDGE INSTEAD OF DRAGON

107. SOUTH ENTRANCE: SPIRIT WAY,
CROSS IN EACH LATTICE

108. IRON TEMPLE GATE, PAINTED
TEMPLE RED

109. CROSS IN WINDOWS

110. SOUTHEAST CORNER AND SUNDIAL

111. SUNDIAL WITH CLOUD DESIGN

112. ALTAR FRONTLET, TWINEM MEMORIAL CHAPEL, UNIVERSITY OF NANKING. Chinese cosmology is based upon the principle of dualism. *Yin* and *yang* are the negative and positive principles of universal life, the two regulating powers which together create all the phenomena of nature. On the even balance of these two ultimate principles depends the well-being of things in heaven and on earth.

On this frontlet, woven in beautiful colors, the *yin-yang* circles have been divided into thirds instead of the usual halves in order to denote the Trinity. In each case the circle is placed against the background of the cross. The Chinese words read "Holy, holy, holy." Between these designs the tapestry has butterflies, birds and fishes woven into it to represent creatures on, above and under the earth glorifying God.

113. A CHINESE SUBSTITUTE FOR ALPHA AND OMEGA. In the chapel (Realm of the Spirit) of the School of Theology, Cheeloo University, Shantung, this medallion is used above the cross on the lectern and on the ends of the pews. The two Chinese characters—with very slight difference in the arrangement of the strokes—are "pen" and "mo," meaning "beginning" and "end." Here they take the place of the Greek letters so common in the West. Compare the appropriateness of this design with what happened in another church where the Greek letters Alpha and Omega were copied *upside down*. Encircling the auditorium as a frieze is the "key" pattern—a symbol of endlessness or eternity. The lectern is an adaptation of a Chinese tea table. The influence of this chapel, designed by Dr. Charles A. Stanley, has been wide and helpful, not alone on the university campus, but also outside, where its motifs and general plan have been copied or adapted in various places.

THE SPIRIT WAY. Many buildings of importance in China have a "Spirit Way" going up to the entrance between steps on either side. This inclined panel is usually a sumptuously designed stretch of marble on which are exquisitely delicate and beautiful carvings of clouds, waves and dragons in low relief. Mythologically this "way" is for the spirits who need no steps, and historically for emperors carried in special chairs above the Spirit Way.

114. On the panel at St. Andrew's Church (*Episcopal*), Wuchang, is a cross against an endless chain as background, two doves of peace—one flying in and the other out—and a grapevine border.

115. The cross rising out of a lotus is the outstanding carving on this architectural feature of the Twinem Memorial Prayer Hall, Nanking. (See Nos. 102-112.) It means here that Buddhism must find completion in the Christ.

116. At the entrance to the administration building of Yenching University is a Spirit Way which shows two struggling dragons.

117. MADONNA, INFANT AND LOTUS. This picture was painted by Tang Yin in the eighteenth century, under the influence of the Jesuits, who introduced many new arts and crafts into China. The Madonna is strongly influenced by the Goddess Kuan Yin, regarded since the Ming dynasty as the Goddess of Mercy and also of Fecundity. The resemblance was supposed to enable the average Chinese better to understand the new personage. An official of the British Museum, where the original of this picture is to be found, writes that the vase and the lotus have Buddhist attributes—the vase containing the water of life, and the opened flower of the lotus in the hand of the child symbolizing enlightenment.

118. A CHASUBLE using Chinese motifs presented by a Chinese ordinand to His Excellency Monsignor Constantini. The phoenix provides a highly decorative design. It is a fabulous bird which, for the Chinese, presides over the southern quadrant of the uranoscope and hence stands for sun, warmth, summer and abundant harvest. Its advent heralds some particularly auspicious event. Early Christians in the West employed it as a symbol of the resurrection. Here it may be merely decorative.

119. THIS PASTORAL STAFF, of South China's typical blackwood, was made for Bishop Mok, a Cantonese and the first Bishop of Canton, by Mr. Yuan Hsi Kuo. The main figure is a copy of the Nestorian cross (Sianfu, A.D. 781). Three of the four points of the cross bear the conventionalized figure of the bat, symbol for happiness and longevity. Underneath, are the cloud design and the lotus whose stalk juts out as the end of the crook of the staff. The staff's head, itself, embodies the plum blossom pattern, another symbol of longevity.

120. "THE HOLY MOTHER AND DIVINE CHILD," a picture by a Chinese artist, is quite fittingly displayed in St. Stephen's Church (*Episcopal*), Manila, a Chinese church. "The Sun of Righteousness" (*Malachi* 4:2) is rising over the horizon to illumine the world, betokening the coming of the Saviour. It speaks of the new life and hope that comes to the Orient through Christ. Below is the baptismal font. The shell that forms the font is locally available and does not necessarily have symbolic significance. In Western symbolism the shell originally was associated with the pilgrims; and frequently the escallop shell, with water dripping from it, has been used as a symbol of our Lord's baptism.

121. CHAPEL, SCHOOL OF THEOLOGY, CHEELOO UNIVERSITY, Shantung. The spaces left by the two crosses on this reading desk in the chapel are filled with the vine and its branches, with fruitage standing out most prominently.

122. THE NESTORIAN CROSS. The famous Nestorian monument, erected in A.D. 781 at Sianfu and, after lying buried, discovered in 1625, tells about the comparatively early introduction of Christianity into China in A.D. 635. In a triangular space near the head of this monument, which is over nine feet high, is the much copied Nestorian cross, reproduced here from a rubbing of the monument. It somewhat resembles that on the reputed tomb of St. Thomas, in India, and like it bursts into *fleurs de lis* at each point. Supporting the cross is the "flying" or "white" cloud—a characteristic symbol of Taoists as well as of Moslems in China. Underneath the cloud is the lotus flower, an emblem of the Buddhists. The Japanese scholar, Professor P. Y. Sacki, thinks that the design was used to show that the three religions were one. Among the various suggested reasons for the disappearance of Nestorian Christianity in China is this and other evidences of a tendency toward syncretism—a confusing of Christianity with Buddhism and Taoism.

123. THIS CROSS (A.D. 960) was found near Peiping at the **Pagoda of the Cross** (Che-tze-seu). In this, also, the cross surmounts the lotus.

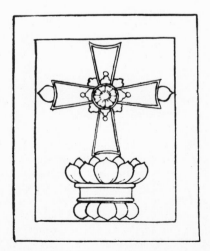

YENCHING UNIVERSITY, Peiping. 124. PAVILION FOR MEDI-
TATION AND RETREATS. The roof beams and eaves of this pavilion are
rich with symbols and decoration. In stiff rows astride the corner hips
sit the protecting lions, or Dogs of Fo. Each end of the roof tiles displays the Chinese character for "all the happiness you wish." In the
squares below these tiles is the swastika in echelon.

125. THE STONE LION. For the last several centuries stone lions have
been characteristic guardians at the gateways of temples or important
public buildings. Originally they were used for the purpose of scaring
demons. The Chinese stone lion is a laughing lion with a curly mane.
There is a tradition that a royal princess first curled her pet lion's
hair and then took him to a lake that he might see his reflection in
the water. Seeing such a beautiful creature made of himself, he burst
into laughter. These lions are delightful reminders of China's old
civilization. Around the base runs the key or meander pattern, without beginning or end, and therefore a symbol of eternity. This picture
is of one of the two lions which stand at the entrance to the campus
of Yenching University, Peiping. A lion sits, also, on either side of
the doorway of the Fitch Memorial Church, Shanghai.

126. THE ALTAR, CATHOLIC UNIVERSITY, Peiping, designed by the Reverend Father Ildephonse of the Benedictine Order.

127

128

CHURCH IN FUKIEN (*A.B.C.F.M.*). 127. THE PULPIT. At the center is a red-lacquered cross. This was such an innovation that it was made only after much consideration ending, however, in unanimous approval. The shade of red used always carries a happy connotation. The circle suggests for this church wholeness, perfectness, completeness, eternity. At the extreme right and left the symbols Alpha and Omega can be seen against a Chinese lattice pattern.

128. COMMUNION TABLE. The most original design on this table is at the center—an Asiatic adaptation of the cross of triumph, signifying the victory of our Saviour over the world. On the circle beneath the cross is a map of Asia. At the extreme left is a bit of the Mediterranean Sea and a bit of eastern Europe, i.e., "the West." A line clearly marks the division between Europe and Asia, showing that Palestine really is not a Western country, but belongs to the Orient. A star marks Bethlehem, and it and its rays are made bright by means of gold leaf. On the extreme right is Japan as another member of the Asiatic family of nations. When one considers how completely Christianity has been identified with Western nationals and Western influence in the minds of the masses of the Chinese, this design appears to have real meaning, and perhaps justification. The problem of including the other nations of the world was considered, for they, too, were recognized as members of the Christian family of nations. But practical considerations obviously made it impossible to show them on this map.

INTERCHURCH SOCIAL CENTER, Hangchow. This beautiful building combines social center and residence for Dr. Robert F. Fitch.

129. TWO DRAGONS in one window are grasping after the priceless pearl, whose sphere typifies the fusing of the two great fundamental principles of *yang* and *yin*.

130. THE GARDEN WALL AND MOON GATE

131. CRANE OF LONGEVITY   132. DEER, THE EMBLEM OF   133. STRUGGLE FOR THE
                                    LONG LIFE   PRICELESS PEARL

134

135

136

137

134. OFFICIAL SEAL OF THE BISHOP OF FUKIEN (*Anglican*). The quarters on the left are symbolic of the missionary work of the mountainous and seaboard diocese of Fukien—the angel with the open Bible flying over the mountains, and the gospel ship carrying the message to the port towns as well as to the islands off the coast.

135. DIOCESE OF HONAN (*Anglican*). On the left are a flaming Oriental lamp and the *fu hsi* (*yin-yang*) diagram (see No. 112). On the right are an open irradiated Bible and three maple leaves.

136. HWA NAN COLLEGE (*Methodist*), Foochow. The flaming torch of truth stands for the college from which the students may light their lamps. In accord with the college motto—"Having received, I ought to give"—the seal symbolizes the influence of Hwa Nan through its alumnae, extending over the mountains and across the sea.

137. ST. JOHN'S UNIVERSITY (*Episcopal*), Shanghai. The bamboo grows very rapidly, and hence the branches in this seal are symbolical of growth. The bamboo, also, suggests serenity—the serenity of academic life and pursuits. The Chinese words were taken from the Confucian "Analects":

Learning without thought is labor lost;
Thought without learning is perilous.

VII : Japan

The question as to whether Japanese symbolism should be used in the decoration of the church and in the accompaniments of worship awakens very little interest among Japanese Christians. Various reasons are assigned. When that remarkable process of absorption of Western culture began in Japan only eighty years ago, Christianity was scarcely differentiated from Western civilization; the Western religion and its Western cultural expressions were taken quite naturally togther. Furthermore, they have no desire, through the suggestions of art, to be reminded of the religion they have left; they have made a clean breach with their religious past. Perhaps they feel instinctively that new wine should be kept in new bottles. The Christian community is relatively small so that the continued strength of their very faith is felt to depend on maintaining a clear-cut apartness.

Without particularly discussing the matter, Japanese seem to feel unconsciously that a Christianity sharply defined from everything that suggests Shinto or Buddhism is the best safeguard for a young church set in vigorous non-Christian surroundings. To adopt or to adapt from older faiths might seem like currying favor or subtle flattery, and might encourage a popular assumption that all religions are more or less the same. Moreover, the Christian community in Japan is largely urban, educated and Westernized, and hence does not chafe under the foreign aspect of Christianity as much as do Christians in certain other countries. Thus for a number of reasons little of the Japanese exquisite sense of harmony and of beauty appears in Christian places of worship.

Much the same attitude is found in Korea. A bishop of Korean Methodism says that "outside a few the Catholics have built, there are no churches in Korea; many meeting houses, but no churches. Commodious enough, comfortable to a degree, but all lacking in beauty." In connection with this study opinions such as the following were expressed: "The Korean church has taken over no symbolism. I have never heard the slightest suggestion that they might even desire to appropriate any native symbolism." "The theory on which the church in Korea **has** gone from the start has been that the new believer makes a complete break with his past and begins an absolutely new life. The use of old symbols would not be considered for a moment, and I think rightly so." "Korean symbolism is about the last thing I should expect to find in any church whose members have an almost complete lack of an artistic sense." "Most symbols have religious or superstitious meanings in Korea and the church will probably not use them." Eddies in the surge of nationalism that lie quite outside the Christian movement, however, may bring reaction against any unnecessary foreignness in the accompaniments of Christian worship.

There is, furthermore, a realm of symbolism that is peculiarly dear to the beauty-loving Japanese—the language of flowers. It has the advantage of being little associated with religion. The bamboo is associated with many worthy sentiments. It is strong and tough, and when bowed down by the weight of snow springs back to its former position—thus should adversity be borne. It splits evenly and shoots up into the sky, signifying a straight and aspiring heart. The plum is the first blossom to appear in Japan, braving the cold and snows of winter; hence this frail flower with its pink, white and yellow buds has long been the theme for moralists and poets, betokening virtue triumphant or valor breaking through benumbing obstacles. The pine, which grows to a very old age, stands for longevity and often appears on wedding decorations or on the bride's kimono. Cherry blossoms, cultivated for a display of half a week and falling just when they are at their best, suggest loyalty and the shedding of one's blood ungrudgingly for a noble cause. Just as the cherry blossom does not cling tenaciously to its branch, so we should not cling to life, if called to give it up in a higher loyalty.

Dr. Nitobé, in his *Japanese Nation,* tells how many a lover of flowers leaves his bed before dawn to hasten to a pond that he may hear the bursting of the lotus buds; and James A. B. Scherer (in *Romance of Japan through the Ages,* p. 102) quotes Fenollosa as saying so beautifully, "To be pure as a plum blossom, free as a bird, strong as a pine, yet pliant as the willow, was the lovely ideal of the Chinese Sung gentleman, as of the later Askikaga Japanese." In fact, each month has some flower or tree in Japan's floral world which for that time is held in especial esteem. It is not surprising, therefore,

104

that many Christian schools in Japan are called by the names of flowers, such as the White Lily School, or Cherry Mountain School in Tokyo. (See also No. 174.) From the pictures that follow it would seem that flowers can be used, not only in the decorative scheme of school or church to give a Japanese flavor to Christianity, but also to emphasize ethical teachings congenial to the faith.

WOMAN'S CHRISTIAN COLLEGE, Tokyo. 138. THE CHAPEL. The walls of this new chapel (1938) are of pre-cast concrete forming a continuous lattice of crosses, diamonds, circles and squares in which glass of forty shades is framed. The huge cross at the altar end stands out in white.

139. THE ALTAR. From right to left the representations are a broken Japanese reed, a lily, and an oak leaf, together symbolizing man's weakness transformed through the resurrection into strength.

To the Japanese the pine, with its cones and fresh needles, symbolizes longevity and consequently good fortune. The highly decorative reeds or rushes, which once grew on the campus as high as ten feet, are associated with autumn. These two motifs are also used in the wall and ceiling lamps of the Administration Building (Nos. 140 and 145) and alternate on the desk lamps of the library (No. 144). The architecture and symbolism throughout are by non-Japanese.

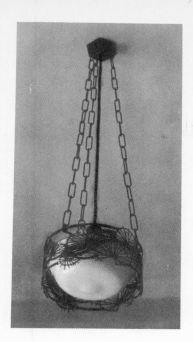

140. CEILING LAMP

141. THE PINE MOTIF ON THE
LIBRARY DOOR

142-143. THE PINE AND RUSH MOTIFS ALTERNATE ON THE LIBRARY'S
BALCONY RAILING

144. DESK
LAMPS

145. HALL LAMP

THE SMITH MEMORIAL CHAPEL, Hikone. Conventional Christian symbols are used in this chapel, but with a Buddhist background; and the various Christian carvings have the general shape and position of Buddhist temple carvings. The building has the curved arch and roof of a Japanese temple, but crosses are shown not only on each ridge, but on each end-tile of the roof (cf. Nos. 149, 150), and in practically every other carving, inside and out. Each of the rafters is tipped with a gold-leaf metal cap. The tables on either side of the altar are exact copies of those used for offerings in a large Shinto shrine.

148. FRONT OF GABLE

149. FRONT ENTRANCE

151. CARVING UNDER ARCH

150. CARVING BELOW GABLE

153. THE CHAPEL DOOR. The four panels represent the pine, chrysanthemum, bamboo, and plum with their symbolic meanings.

152. TILE ABOVE GABLE

154. THE THREE CEILING PANELS above the communion rail have a pattern, partly in carving and partly in scroll-saw work, so that hidden lights shine through the design.

155. A GRAPEVINE PATTERN appears above the wainscoting on either side of the altar alcove.

156. A KAKEMONO (scroll), by the Reverend Shigeyoshi Fukeshima (*Methodist*).

> I am the vine
> Ye are the branches.
> If ye abide in me
> Ye shall bear much fruit.

157. THE CHRISTIAN PILGRIM. This painting by a Presbyterian minister, the Reverend Toshio Saito, symbolizes the life of the Christian pilgrim. The poem above may be translated:

> In shadow and darkness though the road may lie,
> Disciples of the Saviour over it must go.
> Through Hades passes the Living Way.
> Only straight onward will heaven be reached.

THE KIMWHA CHURCH (*Methodist*), Korea. All the motifs used in this interesting church are Korean. One is aware at once it is in and of Korea, not in Europe or America. To right and left in the vestibule are cabinets for the reception of shoes.

158. EXTERIOR. The end of each rafter under the eaves has been decorated with a red five-petaled flower symbolizing for the Koreans the joy and beauty of the Christian life. Each of the little bells that hang in the eaves has a brass fish suspended in the place of a clapper.

159. THE FRONT OF THE CHURCH

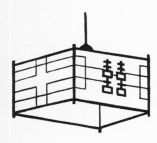

160. THE PULPIT is a Korean cabinet design trimmed with brass, the central figure being a cross of Korean type.

The characters for faith, hope and love on the back of the organ to the right, and for life on the backs of the pulpit chairs (not shown), are given a definitely Christian meaning.

The Reverend V. W. Peters, who designed this church, is planning a communion table that is to be low like all Korean tables to accommodate people sitting on the floor. It is to be lacquered in black and decorated with mother-of-pearl after a fashion common in Korea. The design will probably include the sun symbolizing greatness, warmth, and strength; the crane, for purity; the pine and bamboo, for constancy; as well as appropriate Scripture references.

161. THE LAMPS for the interior carry on their alternate faces the cross and the character for "happiness." The latter character may be seen, also, on the two lamps beside the front door (No. 159).

162. IN THE IRONWORK in front of the glass of the semicircle above each of the three doors in No. 159 can be seen the "flower of eternal youth" symbolizing the renewing of life by Christ. According to tradition this flower must be eaten to be effective—i.e., there must be an individual acceptance of Christ's gifts through faith.

163. THE GLASS in the semicircle above the doors has been painted with ancient designs to resemble stained glass. Above the central door (hardly visible in No. 159) is an adaptation of the fire-cloud motif (A.D. 565) in shades of red and yellow on a cream background, typifying the coming of the Holy Spirit.

164. THE HOLY SPIRIT. Above the two side doors there is a lacquer design (86 B.C.-A.D. 69)—waves of blue with spray of rainbow tints. These two designs together symbolize the cleansing work of the Holy Spirit as fire and water. The symbol of wind is also suggested by the appearance of the flames as being wind-blown.

165. THE PILLARS on either side of the chancel (No. 160) and the beam overhead carry a traditional pattern (A.D. 1650) said to represent dragon scales. Here they are taken to represent fish scales, recalling the early use of the fish in Christian symbolism. At each end of the beam is a pomegranate, the symbol of fruitfulness because of its many seeds—here, the fullness of the Holy Spirit.

166. A VINE MOTIF (not visible in No. 160) runs about the base of the chancel. It was adapted from a mural painting of about A.D. 565, recalling the words about the vine and its branches.

167. DIOCESE OF HOKKAIDO (*Anglican*). The swimming fish typifies the principal industry of Hokkaido. The cross signifies the message of the Christian church. The rising sun stands for Japan (Nippon means "source of the sun").

168. DIOCESE OF KYOTO (*Anglican*). The sun rays behind the mountains signify that the diocese is in the Kingdom of the Rising Sun. The fact that the other symbolism is entirely familiar practically says that "the work of a bishop in the church of God is essentially unchanging throughout all the nations of the world."

169. JAPAN JUNIOR COLLEGE (*Seventh Day Adventist*), Showa-machi. The cherry blossom symbolizes not only Japan itself, but also those ideals of character which the Japanese most respect.

170. KWANSAI GAKUIN UNIVERSITY (*Union*), Nishinomiya. The crescent or new moon has interesting Japanese associations. As the badge of this school and university an attempt is made to reinterpret the crescent moon in the spirit of *Luke* 2:52, as a symbol of growth in body, mind, spirit and social usefulness.

171. PYENG YANG UNION CHRISTIAN COLLEGE (now closed). The central design is associated with the old Korean flag, on which this symbol appears.

172. EWHA COLLEGE, Seoul, Korea. Filling the central portion of the seal is a Korean gateway with its two massive roofs, symbolizing the beauty and the culture of old Korea. It also represents the gate of learning through which the students pass out to fields of opportunity and service. Though the path leads through difficult ways, in the distance may be seen the mountain tops of achievement, which beckon to all who strive through faith and earnestness to attain. The three Chinese characters about the gate are the college motto, "Truth, Goodness, Beauty."

At the top is the *yin-yang* symbol or the Korean *tai-kuk,* a national emblem long dear to the hearts of the people.

At the bottom is the five-petaled pear blossom; for the college name, Ewha, is made up of two words meaning "pear flower." The blossom is white on a green background, signifying that personalities must be pure in their grace and nobility. The green means growth and this must continue endlessly in Ewha students. The meanings of this seal are not forgotten, for the president, Helen K. Kim, sometimes speaks of them in the chapel. It was designed in 1930 by Mrs. Edna Van Fleet Hobbs in association with the president; was revised in 1933; and since then has been greatly simplified by order of the authorities.

173. A KOREAN SUNDAY SCHOOL BANNER, Kimwha Church. This silk embroidered banner is awarded to the class having the largest number of points. The central design is an adaptation of the Korean cross with a crown of the sixth or seventh century. Its three prongs with their three and seven branches respectively represent completion and perfection; and its lacy wings, the power of the Holy Spirit. On the lower arm of the cross is the character for "mountain" thrice repeated standing for the mounts of Beatitudes, Transfiguration and Calvary. The embroidered figures, all in Korean costume, on the right from the bottom up represent Joseph in his coat of many colors, Samuel, and Ruth and Naomi; on the left, Moses playing in the palace with a Korean banner, David, and Daniel. The standard was made by a local carpenter with a cross at the top and with a Korean geometrical design at the base—Christ fulfilling Korean culture.

167

168

169

170

171

172

173

THE PLUM BLOSSOM, which is sometimes so early that it bursts through the snow, represents virtue triumphant, or valor breaking through icy obstacles. In Baiko Jo Gakuin (Plum Blossom School), Shimonoseki, this flower is taken to signify courage, and "life more abundant." It appears on the school uniform (No. 174) and on the official standards such as all schools in Japan have to display when their students, for example, meet famous persons at the station. The little pond in the chapel courtyard, also, is shaped like a plum blossom (No. 175).

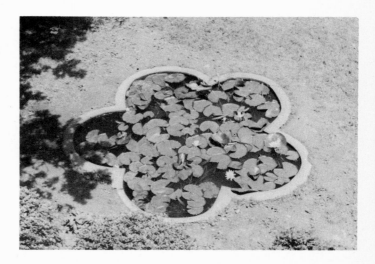

VIII : Africa

The illustrations that follow in this chapter show that here and there can be found examples of meaningful art forms that are African. Such symbols, however, are by no means common. A few quotations from correspondence will throw isolated sidelights on the stage that Christian art in Africa has reached:

"No church that I know has embodied anywhere any Christian symbolism." (Congo Belge.) "The people despise all that is associated with the past. It is something we are continuously trying to correct." (South Nigeria.) "I have not discovered any indigenous symbolism in this part of South Africa. Here the movement to conserve and to encourage African art is recent; and even yet one finds a tendency to encourage artists who are Africans, rather than African art." (Cape Province.) "Christianity is still very new to the people in this part, so that they are still at the stage of taking what is given them rather than bringing their own into the new teaching." (Liberia.) "Here carving or sketching has not been a part of the cultural life of the people." (Nigeria.) "Apart from bodily ornaments and decoration of implements of war, these people have not made artistic expression in material form a strong feature in their culture. Consequently there has been no urge to make churches other than comfortable, or to initiate any European decorations." (Kenya.) "The unfortunate thing with much of the African religious symbols is that they have a degrading significance that will make it almost impossible to use them. There is danger that what is supposed to be African symbolism may really be ideas put into the African mind by a European." (Calabar, West Africa.) "This is a Moslem country and therefore they have no indigenous symbolic drawings—art in this connection being prohibited to them. Art expressing a religious truth is alien to their thought." (Nigeria.) "There is no use of African symbolism in our part of the world. This is partly because the people —remnants of tribes in forest and lagoon areas—are singularly lacking in native art or craft of any sort." (Ivory Coast.)

Other reasons for the absence of African Christian art are suggested by the following: "We have hardly been thinking on these lines." (The Christian Council of South Africa.) "Missions have not encouraged Africans to find a new source of artistic inspiration in Christianity. They have brought bad prints from Europe to illustrate their message and decorate their churches and have given the impression that carving is *juju.*" (*Overseas Education,* Vol. IV, p. 175.) From two areas have come the statements that "our Calvinistic sympathies do not encourage much decoration in our churches."

While these quotations show that probably most missionaries believe that a complete break with the past is essential or inevitable, there are certainly some who firmly believe that the African has an individual contribution to make to the world's culture through his art, and that if the right attitude is taken now he will be able to make this contribution in the future. For such, the guiding principle is that the African should be encouraged to find value in his own artistic point of view and to follow his own artistic traditions. An experienced Roman Catholic, writing about ecclesiastical furnishings, says that "it is rare indeed that a missionary finds himself among peoples so primitive that they do not have a certain ornamental formulary. Decorative motifs are almost always to be found on the spot. There are earthenware vessels, ornaments, textiles, and often bronzes and coppers rich in elements of design." There is danger, however, that Africa's unique contribution will be lost. Commerce with its advertisements and cheap wares, the prestige attached to anything European regardless of its artistic quality, and the infiltration of scientific thought, which alters the mental and emotional basis of African art —all endanger its distinctive development.

Evidently the approach to African art must be a wary one. Undoubtedly many examples can be deeply admired by Europeans on the basis of their own Western standards. There is much art, however, that is evidently admired by the Africans who made it, but which seems ugly or even repulsive to Europeans. This suggests a distinct difference in outlook, which must be taken into consideration.

176. WUSASA CHURCH (*C.M.S.*), Zaria, Nigeria. On the claystone lectern at the right of the chancel may be seen a Hausa (African district) sword-cross, representing "the sword of the Spirit which is the word of God." A window cross is at the back of the chancel.

177. THE BISHOP BULLEN MEMORIAL CHAPEL, BOYS' MIDDLE SCHOOL (*C.M.S.*), Wusasa, Zaria, Nigeria. Another Hausa sword is to be seen carved on the clay and stone lectern to the left, representing "the sword of the Spirit." Since geometrical figures were the only form of art allowed to these people while Moslems, an equilateral triangle symbolic of the Trinity and scarcely to be seen in this picture has been molded on the front of the prayer desk on the right. Forever on their guard against any form of image worship, the customary brass cross of an Anglican church has not been introduced as yet, but three crosses representing Calvary have been modeled on the front of the Holy Table, and cross-windows have been introduced. On the altar cloth of the church has been embroidered a Hausa elliptical design renamed by the Christians a "Hausa cross."

178. THE LIGHT OF THE WORLD. Boys in the C.M.S. school, Benin City, Nigeria, carved this panel after Holman Hunt's picture. It was sold privately.

179. LECTERN in St. Matthew's Church (C.M.S.), Benin City. Near the top of the pedestal an African supports the reading desk in the place of the angel often used in an English lectern.

180. TWO MURAL SHIELDS appear on either side of the central curtain of the Hope Fountain Church (L.M.S.), Bulawayo, S. Rhodesia. On one three blades of wheat are pictured with the words, "The bread of life," in the Sindebele language. On the other is a spray of vine with the words, "The true vine," in Sindebele. The reading above the curtain may be translated, "Praise be to God." The curtain itself, with its cross, was woven in the mission station.

181. WESLEY COLLEGE (*Methodist*), Dumai, Gold Coast. The Ashanti golden stool is a symbol of the soul of Ashantis. The stool, conventionalized, appears in the lowest section of the tower of the college building.

182. THE ASHANTI STOOL appears on the college coat of arms, with the cross on it, showing how one of the aims of the college is to capture the soul of the Ashanti people for Christ.

183. A CARVING IN TEAKWOOD, "The Future of Africa," by Ernest Mancoba, a South African of the Fingo Tribe and a graduate of Fort Hare College.

184-185. WALL PATTERNS, Ankole, Uganda. These patterns molded in mud and painted black and white appear on the walls of a school chapel (C.M.S.). The work was done by local women in the traditional style of wall decoration executed by old women in chiefs' houses.

186. A ZULU PYX. This ebony vessel, surmounted by a cross, was sculptured by a Zulu Roman Catholic to serve as a vessel in which the host or eucharist is preserved.

187. THE CRUCIFIXION, an old ivory carving from Punta Negra, near Loango. Note that our Lord is portrayed as a black man, and the two disciples touching the hem of his garment are also black. This seems to symbolize that, for the artist, the Christ was no foreign white Saviour, but one who had come to him as a black man. No cross is shown, but there are the wounds from invisible nails, and you feel that the cross is behind the outstretched arms. "If genuine feeling, comprehension of a situation, and masterly technique are sufficient to produce a work of lofty dignity, this creation by an unknown savage . . . is a masterpiece in which the tremendous religious feeling and tremendous religious power are combined with singular emotional beauty." This carving is now in the Staatliches Museum für Völkerkunde, Berlin.

DECORATED CHURCH STALLS. 188. THE BENEDICITE. The student carvers at the Diocesan Training College, Pietersburg, N. Transvaal, love to illustrate the Benedicite, the canticle beginning "O all ye works of the Lord, bless ye the Lord." Some of these stalls illustrate "O all ye beasts and cattle, bless ye the Lord." Other stalls are being made representing "O all ye fowls of the air" and "O all ye green things."

189. AN AFRICAN STORY is told on one pew end, which shows a kneeling Bantu drawing his sword of flame, and below a snake coiled about a tortoise. The design was conceived by the Reverend Edward Paterson on the basis of an old African story: God wished man to live forever. But man angered him and he sent the tortoise with a message of death. Repenting, he sent the snake to overtake the tortoise and cancel the death message. The snake dawdled on the way, even heading backwards at times, as in this picture, while the tortoise kept straight on. Thus, man has first to die, and then recover his eternal life.

190. SHEPHERD AND SHEEP

191. VARIOUS OCCUPATIONS OF WOMEN

192. CHAPEL, EVANGELICAL - LUTHERAN MISSION, Sango, Africa.
Erected by Africans in the form of a jungle hut at the instigation of Herrn Missionar
Dr. Bruno Gutmann, this is an example of the second class of symbols (see page 4)—
putting a classical Christian symbol in an indigenous setting.

CRESTS AND SEALS IN AFRICA

193. THE COOPERATION OF BLACKS AND WHITES, the ideal for which the Prince of Wales College, Achimota, Gold Coast, exists, is suggested by this shield. The idea came from a saying of its most gifted and promising teacher, the late Dr. J. E. Kwegyir Aggrey: "You can play some sort of tune on the white keys of a piano; you can play some sort of tune on the black keys; but to produce real harmony you must play both the black and the white keys."

194. DIOCESE OF THE UPPER NILE (*Anglican*), Uganda. Below, against a dark black background, the golden cross and blazing sun betoken the light of the gospel dawning in pagan darkness. The crocodile, very common in the Nile, stands for the power of evil to be conquered through the cross of Christ. Possibly the exigencies of heraldry prevented putting the crocodile in a more appropriate place.

195. DIOCESE OF GEORGE (*Anglican*), Cape Province. The Portuguese, as the first Europeans to come to Cape Province, landed in this diocese; hence the Portuguese warship. The crown represents the monarchy, since in early days the Cape was a Crown Colony. The anchor (hope) symbolizes the Cape of Good Hope.

196. DIOCESE OF LAGOS (*Anglican*), Nigeria. The first Negro bishop of modern times, Samuel Crowther, was consecrated in 1864. Since the oil-palm formed the chief source of wealth in his diocese, he chose this tree, along with the dove and olive branch, for his coat of arms. A later addition (1919) was the altar of sacrifice, indicative of the immense loss of life among the pioneer missionaries in that part of Africa.

197. SOUTH AFRICAN NATIVE COLLEGE (*Union*), Fort Hare, Cape Province. The sun rises out of the darkness of Africa; and the open Bible bears in Latin the words of the psalmist, "In thy light shall we see light."

198. A CONFIRMATION CARD. The Bishop of the Upper Nile had this card prepared for teaching purposes. The hills in the south of the diocese and the two rivers of its plains are symbolically depicted along with the distinctive vegetation and food—the plantain tree in the south and the palm in the north. The young girl and boy look toward the cross, which brings light to their land.

126

193

194

195

196

197

198

IX : Meanings through Symbols of Other People

As members of a world-wide Christian community we have a deep interest in the religious art of each of its constituencies. However, the primary interest of this volume has been in non-Western artistic expressions, partly because of manifest limitations, but also because these non-Western art forms are less well known to the church as a whole. This final chapter must be limited to brief comments and miscellaneous illustrations from various areas.

Throughout the Islamic world (excepting in Iran, whose people have been so artistic as to be obdurate heretics) Islam's ban on the representation of living things has reduced visual art practically to architecture and Arabesque decoration, whether on manuscripts and book covers, or in stucco or other media. This involves a very rich tradition of decoration quite devoid of symbolism. The sense of beauty has been largely expressed through script. The forms of the Arabic alphabet, in themselves very lovely, have been interlaced and used for what can only be described as design.

Although Islam is practically devoid of material symbolism, one should not overlook the impressive way in which in a mosque, at prayer, the *imam* and the whole congregation in serried rows turn, literally, toward Mecca; but for the more devotionally minded it is a turning of one's whole being to God. The late Canon Gairdner felt that converts from Islam might miss this impressive and symbolic common facing of leader and people for the great affirmations of their faith. When, therefore, in the Christian service, the recitation of the Creed occurred, he always left the reading-desk to stand in front of the first row of people, facing the same way as the congregation.

An interested and experienced missionary writes that "it is disappointing that most of the missions of the Near East have interpreted their religion as involving a terrible bareness and ugliness. All historical tradition except that of the Reformaton in the West has been largely ignored. This has its strong effect on the lives of Near East-

128

ern Protestants. One can sense that they are missing something that ought to be theirs."

Interesting initiative, however, has been taken in various places. The Coptic church in Egypt has many decorated crosses dating from about the fifth century and used as consecration crosses on ancient early Christian pulpits. Copies of these old crosses have been introduced as the carved decoration for wooden church furniture to the great pleasure of members of this ancient church. In one Christian Arabic congregation the old Egyptian "sign of life" (Ankh), or Cross Ansata (shown minutely in No. 210), appears along with the Jerusalem cross on an embroidered curtain, thus symbolizing union in the Cross, or more particularly in this congregation the union of Egyptian and Palestinian Christians. In the Gairdner Memorial Church at Old Cairo there is an adaptation of an ancient Coptic design in which the date palm and the pomegranate (two of the most natural signs of fruitfulness) issue from a vase marked by a cross.

There are two stimulating examples where a symbolic token has been presented by a younger to a parent church—from Iran (No. 202), and from Thailand (Siam) (No. 204). Other examples of the use of Christian symbolism in the Near East and in certain other areas are given in the pages that follow.

129

CHURCH OF ST. SIMON THE ZEALOT (*Anglican*), Shiraz, Iran. Notice the prevailing geometrical designs in this church. Floral designs, also, are used in neighboring mosques, but the geometrical designs were selected as conveying a greater sense of majesty and dignity.

199. THE CHANCEL. The cross on the reredos or panel above the altar is shown filling the space under a double depressed Persian arch, betokening the permeation of Persia by Christianity. The extended arch pattern has been copied from one encircling a minaret in Azerbaijan.

200. THE BAPTISTRY. Above the font in the baptistry, between the tops of the windows, a copy of the Nestorian cross can be seen. It is in colored tiles. The pearls attached to the arms of the cross were originally Buddhistic symbolism. Here they suggest the clear translucent pearl-like lives produced by contact with the Crucified One.

201. THE VINE AND BRANCHES in this picture indicate what our Lord is saying to the group before him. The artist, Hosein Behzad-Miniateur of Teheran, is one of the best living Iranian painters. He is a member of the Evangelical Church of Teheran, and would like to give all his time to painting Christian subjects in the true Iranian tradition.

202. A PLAQUE WITH ECUMENICAL ASSOCIATIONS. The universal and interpenetrating character of Christianity is well illustrated by this engraved silver plaque, somewhat blurred in reproduction by the many reflections from its shining surface. It was made in Iran, presented by Iran's Church of Christ to a sister church in America, and embodies symbolism from China introduced there by Christians from the Near East.

The design was drawn by Hosein Behzad-Miniateur, a nationally known painter in Iran and recently converted to Christianity. Two of the wise men are shown on camels on the right. The star above is shining through the scattered clouds of Islam and illuminates the cross. The three rings on each arm of the cross represent the Trinity.

The symbolism on the left was consciously taken from the Nestorian stone tablet, carved in China, A.D. 781, and discovered in Sianfu after being covered with sand for centuries. On the Chinese tablet the cross is resting upon a lotus leaf symbolizing Buddhism. But since Iran is not a Buddhist country, the lotus leaf is replaced by the *foruhar* (wings of Ahura Mazda) to represent Zoroastrianism. There are some flowers growing on each side symbolizing that beauty springs up wherever the cross is planted.

This silver plaque was presented by the Church of Christ in Iran to the Board of Foreign Missions of the Presbyterian Church, U. S. A., at its centennial anniversary in 1937.

203. A SYMBOL OF INTERCULTURAL SYMPATHY. One purpose in building the Oriental Hall at the American University, Cairo, Egypt, was that it should be an instrument of service—a meeting place for leaders in the thought life of Egypt. It is, also, a challenge—it calls East and West to collaborate in works of research and study. In addition, the dedication pamphlet (1932) says that "first and foremost, it is a symbol. Inspired by the generous impulses of American donors, yet expressing itself in lines of Oriental beauty and art, it is a symbol of international and interracial sympathy; more than that, of intercultural sympathy. It expresses the friendship of America for Egypt. On its walls are inscribed great names that reveal how Greek and Hebrew, Moslem and European minds and hearts have labored to place the richest values of the Orient at the disposal of the world."

204. FROM A YOUNGER TO A PARENT CHURCH. In 1937 the National Christian Church of Thailand (Siam), through its moderator, sent a teakwood cross, almost three feet high, flanked by two Siamese elephants, to the United Church of Hyde Park, Chicago. In Eastern Asia the elephant stands for strength, energy, sagacity and prudence as well as for gentleness and meekness. In bulk and strength, the elephant is inferior to none; however, it displays no arrogance. The animal is sacred to Buddhism, which emphasizes tenderness of disposition in all its followers. The Siamese have adopted the White Elephant as their national emblem.

This symbolic token was designed by a Korean architect, and executed by a Siamese workman. The Chicago church had for some decades supported missions in Siam, and a close relationship had been maintained. It was hoped that this Siamese cross would be the means of linking together more vitally Christians in Siam and America. "It gives me much pleasure," wrote the moderator, "to realize that Siamese workmanship is to assist the members of your church in making our common Christ more real."

205. A COMMUNION SET. That communion vessels have secondary connotations that may be easily overlooked was discovered by the Reverend J. R. Richards of Shiraz, Iran. For years an English communion set had been used to the apparent satisfaction of all. But some time ago he ordered a set embodying beautiful native work. He was amazed at the difference it made. Western art, even as Western music, made little appeal to this congregation. But they loved their own beautiful native art, and it brought out the best in them.

206. AMERICAN FARM SCHOOL, Thessalonica, Greece. The sower is a fitting symbol for a school teaching new methods of farming in an arid country. For them to work is literally to pray (cf. motto). Moreover, the school believes that its three hundred graduates are sowing another kind of seed even more important and far-reaching for good in the Balkans.

207. ANATOLIA COLLEGE (*A.B.C.F.M.*), Saloniki, Greece. Every morning the sun illumines the profile of a large mountain near the college. The motto that always accompanies the seal is from the words of Isaiah, "The morning cometh," and is the symbol of faith and hope that has triumphed over pessimism and despair through all the years that the college has served the peoples of the Near East.

The college has established in its main building a little Orthodox church with its candles, its icons, its vestaments and its cross. Every Sunday morning they use the liturgy of St. Chrysostom under the leadership of an Orthodox priest. They have found in this service a medium of expression for their student body more useful than the less symbolic Western service.

208. AMERICAN UNIVERSITY OF BEIRUT, Beirut, Lebanon. The tree on this seal (adopted in 1920) represents a cedar of Lebanon. In traditional Christian symbolism the cedar of Lebanon, on account of its height, its healing qualities, and the incorruptibility of its core, suggests grandeur, dignity and bounty.

209. THE AMERICAN UNIVERSITY, Cairo, Egypt. The star and the sphinx in this seal symbolize Egypt bathed in the light of the star of Christianity.

210. ASSIUT COLLEGE (*United Presbyterian*), Assiut, Egypt. The library seal is set against a balance as background. In the scale to the left is a feather, ancient hieroglyphic symbol for truth. On the extreme right is a canopic jar, hieroglyphic symbol for the soul or heart. Thus this balance symbolizes the college motto, which appears at the center in English and in Arabic. The English lettering in its style is reminiscent of the ancient Coptic. Immediately above the motto is the winged disk of the sun—the Egyptian god, Re. At the left of the motto is the flower of Lower Egypt (papyrus); and at the right the flower of Upper Egypt (lily), taken from the Thutmoside pillar at Karnak. At the bottom, separating the dates 1865 in the two languages, are three crosses—the Crux Ansata or Key of Life, of ancient Egyptian origin, on the left; the Latin cross in the middle; and a Coptic cross on the right. In designing this seal (adopted in 1939) an attempt was made to combine symbols from ancient Egypt, Coptic Egypt, and from Western Christianity.

211. DIOCESE OF EGYPT AND THE SUDAN (*Anglican*). St. Mark was the first bishop of the Christian church in Egypt, and the church in Abyssinia and the Sudan came under the jurisdiction of the Coptic patriarch of Alexandria about the fourth century. Hence, above, the Lion of St. Mark flanked by the two Coptic crosses. Below is the Nile winding its way from the lakes down to the Mediterranean Sea, and on the left side of the bank is a pyramid and a sphinx. Beneath the shield is a crown and two palm leaves, since the dedication of the diocese is to All Saints.

206

207

208

209

210

211

THE MAKIKI CHRISTIAN CHURCH, Honolulu. 212. EXTERIOR. As one result of the early work started by Francis Xavier and his fellow-Jesuits in Japan, Lord Hisahide Matsunaga became a Christian; and, in 1560, erected a "Place-to-worship-Lord-of-Heaven." A castle stands for grandeur and security. Furthermore, in Christian usage a high tower betokens God's protecting care. Each of these symbolic thoughts lay back of the choice of architecture in this modern church of Honolulu.

The pastor who created this symbolism and who still serves this church writes, "I am working with the earnest hope of producing out of Hawaiian-born Japanese—'Japanese' in racial origin and by outward appearance—citizens of this country with a strong character like a mighty castle and with a truly Americanized and Christianized spirit. This, I believe, should be our contribution to America."

213. TWO GILDED DOLPHINS may be detected at either end of the highest ridgepole in No. 212. Here, as often in Japan, the symbol of the fish is used in its early Christian significance.

214. CEILING. Japanese love flowers, and Buddhists decorate the walls and altars of their shrines with sacred flowers. It was natural, therefore, for this Japanese church to have the flowers of Japan and Hawaii painted in the various ceiling squares.

216. ENTRANCE TO LOGGIA

217. THE MUSIC TOWER   218. THE DOOR

THE CHURCH OF THE CROSSROADS, Honolulu. Those who designed the Church of the Crossroads in 1936 wished it to symbolize the cultural blending actually in process in the congregation. Hence there are intentional suggestions of Polynesian, Chinese and Japanese motifs. There is wood from the Philippines and Samoa. The rich red columns and beams of the connecting loggias (No. 216) impart a Chinese element to the building. Recognition of the fact that the church is located in Hawaii is found in the wooden entrance doors (No. 218), showing the natural grain of the monkey-pod. The doors are flanked by bas-reliefs in stone of the *pandanus* or *lauhala*, which is so important in the life of Hawaiians because its fruit is edible and its long, spear-like leaves are woven into many articles of usefulness. This design carries, also, the old symbolism of the Tree of Life, and in this case the roots are peculiarly braced in all directions against storms and stresses, thus giving the feeling of rootedness.

The light gray-green cast-stone work which decorates each corner (Nos. 215, 216) and runs up the sides of the Music Tower (No. 217) represents the banana leaf and flower, thus tying the building into the Hawaiian garden landscape with its profuse growth.

The Music Tower (No. 217) is surmounted by a gilded cross, below which are three sets of triple concentric rings representing perfection and eternity.

The four buildings constituting the church all face inward to a courtyard, away from the noise and distractions of the busy street, symbolizing that instruction, crafts, social life and administration are all integrated with worship. (See also Nos. 14-18.)

219. LAMP AND BACKGROUND in carved
wood, East Java. "I am the Light of the World"
(*John* 8:12).

220. CARVED PULPIT, Blitar, East Java

221. CHRIST AT THE DOOR. We wish to end this volume with the well-known symbol of *Revelation* 3:20, as painted with spiritual feeling by Mr. Lu Hung Nien of the Catholic University, Peiping. This theme of Christ's approach to the human soul is a favorite one, both in the East and in the West, a fact that suggests that more and more the whole world is hearing a voice saying, "Behold, I stand at the door and knock."

FRONTISPIECE

222. A REREDOS, Blitar, East Java. The design of this cloth screen dyed in white and red on a background of dark blue, symbolizes our Lord's victory. At the bottom is a globe (the world and humanity). The world lies in darkness enveloped in sin (symbolized by flames on either side of the globe). But the Prince of Light, represented by the cross on the Golgotha hill, has come illumining the world and bruising the head of the serpent (sin, cf. *Genesis* 3:15). The large wings on either side suggest the cherubim covering the mercy seat (*Exodus* 25:20, 22), and are intended to remind worshippers that God is always ready to be near, to hear, and to speak. All this is possible through the Holy Spirit (the bird flying over the cross). The bird has eleven wing feathers (the disciples), seven tail feathers, and three head feathers (the Trinity). Back of the whole is the thought of *Hebrews* 10. The design was suggested by a missionary, but the symbolism is truly Javanese, the details being worked out by a Javanese teacher, Noerdja Setja; and the batik-work done by a skillful woman of Modjowarna—both Christians.

Index

148

149

150